THE OFFICIAL OLYMPICS TRIPLECAST VIEWER'S GUIDE

A SERVICE OF NBC & CABLEVISION

1992 BARCELONA
COMMEMORATIVE EDITION

PINDAR PRESS

Publisher **Harvey Rubin**
Editor **Michael Rosenthal**
Creative Director **Joan Walton**
Associate Editor **Cathy Sylvis**
Contributing Editor **Joe Guise**
Research Assistant **John Shabe**

Executive V.P. Marketing **Richard Brescia**
Director of Marketing **Bernard Roberts**
Account Executive **Michael Marchand**
Administrative Director **Sonja Léobold**
Administrative Assistant **Alice Federico**

◆

Pindar Press gratefully acknowledges the help and cooperation of the following individuals and organizations.

Olympics TripleCast: Martin C. Lafferty, Vice President, Olympics TripleCast. **Vice Presidents:** William E. Berman, Network Services · Ellen M. Cooper, Public Relations · Terry S. Freedman, Administration · Stephen R. Lake, Consumer Services · David N. Meyer, Business Affairs · Barbara J. Parsky, Sponsor Services. **Regional Vice Presidents, Affiliate Services:** J. Starrett Berry, Southwest · William R. Cigich, Central · Mark Henderson, Southeast · Louise D. Henry, West · Alan S. McDonald, North Central · Kathryn N. Strachan, Northeast. **Regional Directors, Affiliate Services:** Jacyn Cline, Southwest · Nancy R. Cramer, Northeast · Thomas Fennell, Southeast · Victoria L. Kent, West · Richard T. Steele, North Central · Gail M. Wehling, Central. **Administrative Staff:** Linda A. Grillo, Nikki M. Pesusich, Virginia J. Romagnola, Daniel H. Schmerzler, Jacqueline W. Van Weeren.

NBC: Peter Diamond, Vice President, Olympic Programming · Brett Goodman, Molly Solomon, Olympic Research · Maria Pagano, Manager, Olympic Archives.

The United States Olympic Committee, International Olympic Committee, The Athletics Congress, U.S. Baseball Federation, USA Basketball, USA Amateur Boxing Federation, United States Diving, Inc., U.S. Equestrian Team, U.S. Gymnastics Federation, U.S. Soccer Federation, U.S. Swimming, Inc., U.S. Synchronized Swimming, Inc., U.S. Tennis Association, U.S. Volleyball Association, United States Water Polo, USA Wrestling.

◆

Design Consulting **Twelve Point Rule**
Paper **Champion International**
Lithography **Quad/Graphics, Inc.**

© 1991 Pindar Press / NBC Inc.

ISBN 0-918223-91-1
Library of Congress Catalogue Card Number 91-067265

Overlooking Barcelona, the sculptured performers of the Sardana, a ritual folk dance, celebrate the unity of the Catalonian people.

CONTENTS

THE PASSIONATE SPECTATOR
George Plimpton
4

CHAMPIONS
Brian Cazeneuve
17

ATHLETICS - TRACK
James Dunaway
34

ATHLETICS - FIELD
James Dunaway
44

BASEBALL
Vic Ziegel
52

BASKETBALL
Larry Eldridge
54

BOXING
Michael Shapiro
60

DIVING
Sharon Robb
64

EQUESTRIAN
Nancy Jaffer
68

GYMNASTICS
Kent Hannon
70

RHYTHMIC GYMNASTICS
Dwight Normile
76

SOCCER
Paul Gardner
78

SWIMMING
John Powers
80

SYNCHRONIZED SWIMMING
Barbie Ludovise
86

TENNIS
John Weyler
88

VOLLEYBALL
Jonathan Lee
94

WATER POLO
Michele Himmelberg Farmer
100

WRESTLING
John Husar
102

RECORDS AND STATISTICS
106

EDITOR'S NOTE

In this guide we refer to the current national team of the former Soviet Union as representing the Commonwealth of Independent States (C.I.S.). Publication deadlines precluded addressing the possibility of the independent Republics fielding their own teams.

THE PASSIONATE SPECTATOR

George Plimpton attends twelve centuries of the Olympic Games

The Discobolus, attributed to Myron. The ancient Greek sport of discus throwing was reinvented for the first modern Games in 1896.

Who has not wanted to be *there* in moments of great drama or consequence, sometimes to such a degree we actually convince ourselves that we *were* there. Hundreds of thousands have described themselves sitting in the Polo Grounds and watching Bobby Thomson hit the home run ("The Shot Heard 'Round the World") that beat the Dodgers on the last day of the 1951 season. Wilt Chamberlain once told me that countless fans had seen him score 100 points against the New York Knicks in Madison Square Garden, when in fact the game was played in a rather small arena in Hershey, Pennsylvania.

But no matter. It is a pleasant exercise to imagine oneself sitting on the edge of a seat at an event famous for an expression of athletic prowess at its best. What better venue than the Olympics? Every four years they absorb not only one's attention but one's imagination. At those times, as the columnists recall past glories, and the histories of the Games are in the bookstores, it is impossible to read such things about the Olympics — ancient or modern — without the forlorn wish: If only I could have been on hand to watch *that!*

GIVEN THE CHOICE, SURELY I WOULD LIKE TO TRAVEL BACK in time for a glimpse of the ancient Games at Olympia in western Greece. They spanned an astonishing length of time — from 776 B.C. until the late fourth century A.D., when Theodosius I, a Christian emperor of Rome, had them not only discontinued (he considered them pagan rites) but evidence of them destroyed. Until their demise, the Games were held every four years, just as they are today, and always on the same site at Olympia. Heralds and messengers went the length of the land proclaiming the event; just about everything stopped for the Games, even wars. A one month "sacred truce" on either side of the Games was observed. Noting this, Baron Pierre de Coubertin, who founded the modern Games, lamented that while in ancient days wars

George Plimpton, founder and editor of the Paris Review, *has written numerous bestsellers, including* Paper Lion, Shadow Box *and* The Bogey Man. *His most recent book is* The Best of Plimpton.

stopped for the Games, in the 20th century the Games stopped for wars.

In the Olympics' earliest days the only event was a race the length of the stadium. Not much to see there. All was over in one day. But eventually, enough events — the discus, javelin, broad jump, boxing, wrestling, the pentathlon and chariot racing, among them — were added to lengthen matters to five days.

Depiction of a foot race on a black-figured Greek vase, c. 530 B.C.

THE MEN IN THE ANCIENT GAMES PERFORMED NAKED and oiled. Women were not allowed to compete, or even watch, except for the priestesses of Demeter. The penalty if caught inside the arena was extremely severe — death by being tossed off a cliff. A number of instances are recorded of women, usually mothers, defying the rule to see their offspring perform. The mother of Pisidorus, a young racer, disguised herself as a trainer to get into the arena. Her enthusiasm at her son's victory was such that her disguise fell away and she was apprehended. In this particular case, the authorities took the relationship between the two into account and the mother was spared. As a consequence, trainers also had to strip naked to close off that form of disguise.

The situation eventually changed, of course. At the 128th Olympic Games, the winning driver of chariots drawn by four colts was a woman, Belische of Macedonia.

THE HIGH-BORN OCCASIONALLY CHOSE TO TAKE PART IN the Games. But such a priority was put on winning (competitors prayed for either "the wreath or death") that often it didn't seem worth the risk. Philip II of Macedon won three equestrian events at Olympia, but his son, Alexander the Great, refused to compete, though an accomplished athlete and horseman. He announced that he would participate "only if kings will be my opponents." As a commanding general, he felt the word "defeat" was appropriate only to a battlefield.

Such a consideration may well have been in Nero's mind when the Roman emperor came to Olympia in 67 A.D. He had no intention of losing. He had 5,000 supporters on hand, such an intimidating crowd that he was able to force his will on the authorities. At his instructions, special events were introduced, including a ten-horse chariot race and musical contests. It was arranged that he win all of them — best singer, best herald, best musician (ah, that famous fiddle — actually a lyre) and the best chariot-driver. The chariot race turned out to be more taxing than he expected. In the middle of it he tumbled out onto the course — at which time his competition reined in its horses and waited for him to get back into his chariot. (Some writers claim that a new driver had to take over, but it is not worth arguing about. The point clearly was to ensure that Nero's chariot crossed the finish line first, which it apparently did.)

But I absolutely would have put those 67 Games on my list, if only to catch a glimpse of the fellow….

Engraving of an Olympic champion entering the Temple of Zeus.

Two events I would especially like to have seen back in the ancient Games are the broad jump (known today as the long jump) and the high jump — these to solve a puzzle involving gadgets the competitors carried in their hands called halteres or jumping weights. Made of lead, stone or marble, they weighed between two and eight pounds. Their function was to improve the jumper's performance. Carrying them in both hands, the jumper swung them in an arc so that at the takeoff point he was pulled along above the ground (or up, in the case of the high jump) astonishing distances and heights. Part of the trick was to let go of the weights in mid-flight. Almost all the painted panels on the vases that preserve so much of the history of the ancient Games show the jumpers carrying halteres of various sizes and shapes.

The definitive histories I have read about the Olympics mention the halteres, usually without question. In one of them, E. Norman Gardiner's *Athletics of the Ancient World*, the author cites the performance of a Mr. A. J. Howard who allegedly jumped 29'7" at Chester in 1854, using five-pound dumbbells and taking off from a board two feet long and three inches thick — a leap almost five inches longer than Bob Beamon's extraordinary jump in the 1968 Mexico City Games. As for the high jump, Gardiner reports that R.H. Baker cleared 6'8¼" inches at Leeds, July 14, 1900. A man named Darby cleared 6'5½" inches at Wolverhampton, February 5, 1892, using eight-pound weights which he tossed away in mid-flight.

Highly doubtful! No matter how ferocious an upward swing of the arms, it's hard to imagine anyone carrying a total of 16 pounds getting more than a couple of feet off the ground. I tried it with two rocks in my hands, jumping up from the terrace stones with a great grunt; I got about five inches into the air and scared my daughter's cat.

Eventually, I called an authority at Yale University, Professor Robert Adair, a physicist and author of the delightful volume *The Physics of Baseball*. Professor Adair, who knows how baseballs curve in the air, felt that a performer could be helped, if slightly, with weights, specifically in the standing jump, an event since discontinued in the modern Olympics. He mentioned what he called a "useful transfer of energy." Incidentally, the record for the standing jump (without halteres) is just under 12 feet.

I also called the Olympic Training Center in Colorado Springs, where performance standards and potentials are stored in computers. "Ah yes," I was told. "We have what you want right here." I could hear the rustling of pages being turned. "Roberto Quercetani, the Italian authority ... the most up-to-date source. Here's what he writes:

'J. Howard jumped 29'7" at Chester in 1854 using five-pound dumbbells....' "

To judge for myself, I would like to attend an actual performance with the halteres, perhaps to see Phayllus of Croton do the broad jump. A famous athlete mentioned by Pausanias, Herodotus and Plutarch among others, he is said (according to an epigram on his statue at Delphi) to have jumped (with the aid of halteres, of course) 55 feet! Even the historians draw the line here, equating the feat with other similar hyperbolic legends such as the one about Milo, the athlete who carried a four-year-old heifer around the track at Olympia and then sat down and ate it at a single meal!

Athletes and trainers practicing with halteres on a red-figured vase, c. 520 B.C.

Woodcut of an Olympic victor returning in triumph to his native town.

torious athletes, similar expressions of adulation for the triumphant would hardly appeal to today's poets. I will always remember the last marathon runner coming into the Coliseum in the Los Angeles Games — a Haitian with the lovely, poetic name, Dieudonne Lamothe — and that he received as joyous a reception from that enormous throng as had been given the Portuguese runner who won the race.

THE MODERN OLYMPIC GAMES, ESTABLISHED BY BARON Pierre de Coubertin, were first held in Athens in 1896. Just for tradition's sake, it would have been appropriate to watch the first person actually to be awarded a medal: James Connolly, a Harvard undergraduate. He paid his own way to Athens, one of 285 athletes representing 13 countries. He won the event then known as the hop, step and jump, now referred to as the triple jump. For his victory he received a medal and an olive wreath. The American flag was hoisted on a flagpole and a band played the National Anthem — a tradition that has lasted to this day — to the dismay of some who believe the Olympics should honor individuals, not countries.

Although Connolly always remembered his Olympic experience providing him with the greatest moments of his life, Americans back home did not care one way or another about the results in Greece. Connolly was engagingly rueful about what happened to him on his return. He arrived in Boston with eleven cents in his pocket. No one was there to meet him. Alone, he decided to celebrate. One could do a lot with eleven cents in those days. He had himself a soda. For two cents he bought a newspaper — perhaps to see if there was anything in it about his victory in Greece. There wasn't. He used his last nickel to take the trolley home. He was dropped off near it. The conductor helped him off with his suitcases.

ONE CRITICAL DISTINCTION EXISTS BETWEEN THE ANCIENT and the modern Games — namely the spirit in which they have been played. For Pindar, the greatest lyric poet of the fifth century B.C., the essential quality for an athlete of his time was expressed by the word *aidōs*, a kind of code to which the athlete should adhere — a feeling of respect, reverence, modesty, honor: qualities which distinguish the athlete from the bully.

And yet *aidōs* had very little to do with sportsmanship. In the ancient Games there were prizes for coming in second, third and so on (tripods, amphoras of oil, cauldrons), but there was never the tradition of shaking hands after a competition; winners were never congratulated by those they had beaten. Losers were looked upon with disdain, their home towns disgraced. Pindar wrote of them: "By back ways they slink away sore smitten by misfortune. No sweet smile greets their return."

While a strong tendency to over-emphasize winning has always existed, our present-day culture has never lost its compassion for the also-ran (except perhaps at the racetrack) — a concept that came in with Christianity and its concern for the meek. While Pindar wrote forty-five odes celebrating vic-

Pierre de Coubertin, founder of the modern Olympic Games.

Spiridon Louis won the first marathon in 1896 by more than seven minutes.

A NUMBER OF THE LONG-DISTANCE RACES, ESPECIALLY the marathon, would have been interesting to drop in on — though they were not run in the ancient Games, which did not hold foot races longer than 4,800 meters. The marathon was introduced in the first modern Games in Athens; in fitting circumstance it was won by a Greek named Spiridon Louis, a shepherd who allegedly got his legs in shape by running alongside his mules as they hauled water and mail in the villages around Athens. Forty years later, in 1936, Louis, a sprightly 64-year-old dressed in national costume and carrying his country's blue and white flag, led the athletes into the Berlin Olympic stadium, past Adolf Hitler's box of honor. Before the Games were over, he presented Hitler with a laurel wreath from Olympia. Louis died in 1940; one year later his country came under German occupation.

The second marathon, in 1900, is worth mentioning, though it's not likely I or anyone else would have seen much of it. Beginning and ending in the Bois de Boulogne, the race was laid out through the back streets of Paris in a course so confusing to the runners that 11 of the 19 starters simply gave up, many of them presumably repairing to the nearest bistro. Michel Théato, a Parisian baker, won the race, but he was accused of taking shortcuts through alleys only he as a Frenchman would know; it was ten years before the International Olympic Committee finally confirmed that he was indeed the winner.

The St. Louis marathon, four years later, was also rife with controversy. An American runner, Fred Lorz, finished first, and Alice Longworth, Teddy Roosevelt's daughter, draped a laurel wreath around his neck. He was about to receive the first-place medal, when it was discovered that he had, in fact, collapsed after about nine miles in the 102-degree heat and been picked up by a car. When the car itself collapsed in the heat some miles from the finish, Lorz, quite refreshed by now, started running again. He hit the tape so far in advance of anyone else that I can't believe he didn't accept the wreath in a spirit of puckishness. American track officials were not delighted, however, and he was immediately banned for life from competing in any authorized races. (He was later reinstated and won — legitimately — the 1905 Boston Marathon.)

What a strange cast of characters ran in that St. Louis race! One of the starters was Felix Carvajal, a Cuban mailman. He had raised funds on his own in the squares of Havana, but had promptly lost his stake in a gambling den in New Orleans. Arriving in St. Louis penniless, he turned up at the starting line in his mailman's regalia, including a pair of heavy boots. As he ran he began shedding his clothes; he ate apples and peaches along the way, and on occasion lay down at the roadside to rid himself of stomach cramps. He arrived at the finish line in his underwear — a surprising fourth. The man who won the race, Thomas Hicks, had a doctor in attendance who from time to time gave him painkillers and doses of brandy accompanied by infusions of strychnine sulfate mixed with raw egg white.

The London marathon, four years later, was even more bizarre. The entire Olympics was played out against a background of intense anti-American feeling, most of it engendered when the athlete carrying the American flag declined to dip it while marching past the royal box in the opening ceremonies. American Johnny Hayes was favored to win the race, but to everyone's surprise, the first to enter the Olympic Stadium was a diminutive Italian in long, black shorts named Dorando Pietri, a pastry cook by profession. Dazed from exhaustion and the heat, he turned the wrong way on the track. An English official, fearing that the despised American, Hayes, was coming into the stadium behind Pietri, rushed out and turned him around, rather like a stalled toy, to get him going again in the right direction. After a few steps Pietri collapsed, at which point other officials (including Arthur Conan Doyle, a great track enthusiast!) came out and practically carried Pietri across the finish line. This was too much even for the officials; however prejudiced they were against the Americans at that time, they eventually disqualified Pietri and pronounced Hayes the winner.

But that's one finish I would like to have seen — if only for the chance to jostle around and perhaps hobnob with Sir Arthur!

It was in London, incidentally, that the distance the marathon is now run (26 miles, 385 yards — or 42.195 kilometers) was established. Most people, I among them, had always thought it was the distance run by Pheidippides in 490 B.C. to bring news of the victory over the Persians on the Plains of Marathon, and who had dropped dead after shouting, or murmuring more likely, "Rejoice, we conquer!" Not at all. The distance run in Athens in 1896 was a conjectured 24-odd miles. But in 1908 the distance was laid out between the steps of Windsor Castle and the royal box in the Olympic Stadium outside London. This was done so King Edward's and Queen Alexandra's grandchildren could watch the start from the steps, perhaps before their afternoon naps, and that has been the distance for the marathon ever since.

Dorando Pietri is about to collapse as he nears the finish line of the 1908 marathon.

He was once asked if he thought of himself representing Finland when he raced.

"I ran for myself, never for Finland."

"Not even in the Olympics?"

"Not even then. Above all, not even then. At the Olympics, Paavo Nurmi mattered more than ever!"

The Finns apparently did not take exception to this sentiment. When the 76-year-old Nurmi died in 1973, the government gave him a state funeral. A statue of Nurmi stands near the Olympic Stadium in Helsinki.

AS FOR THE MORE SUCCESSFUL DISTANCE RUNNERS, I certainly wouldn't have passed up the chance in the 1920s to watch Paavo Nurmi, the Flying Finn. As a youngster, Nurmi trained by chasing trolley cars in the city and mail trains through the deep, pine forests. He was one of the first to systematize his races, checking his laps with a watch. He was a taciturn, stolid, huge-chested man with an enlarging bald spot. My friend Jim Murray, the *Los Angeles Times* columnist, once described him as "sere as the Finnish winter, as bleak as an icicle, as gloomy as the second act of an Ibsen play." He ran a variety of distance races, even the mile, but his specialties were the 5,000 and 10,000 meters. By the time he retired after the Amsterdam Olympics in 1928, he had won nine gold and three silver medals. He had very definite views about the role of the individual in the Olympics.

Paavo Nurmi, the "Flying Finn," in the 1920 Olympics.

Trailing his Finnish countryman Ville Ritola in the 10,000 meters in 1928, Paavo Nurmi took the lead with 150 meters to go and set a new Olympic record by over four seconds.

Jesse Owens, whose four gold medals dominated the 1936 Olympics.

WHAT A PRIVILEGE IT WOULD HAVE BEEN TO SEE JIM Thorpe and Jesse Owens, two of America's greatest athletes of the first half of the 20th century, perform in their respective Olympics. Thorpe's was Stockholm in 1912. A native American, he was one of the legendary figures of the modern Games. His career started at the Carlisle Indian School in Pennsylvania where he played football. His coach was "Pop" Warner, after whom the American boys' football program is named. At Carlisle, Warner's ill-manned football squad (16 players) was one of the best in the country. During 1911-12, when Thorpe was an all-American, Carlisle went 23-2-1, beating powerhouses like Army, Harvard, Penn and Pitt.

In Stockholm, Thorpe won the pentathlon and the decathlon, both decisively. In addition to his gold medals, King Gustav V presented him, as hero of the Games, with a bronze bust and a bejeweled Viking ship. Thorpe is supposed to have said, though it is unlikely, "Thank you, King." I would have liked to have been there to check it out.

Eventually, of course, it was revealed that Thorpe had received sixty dollars a month playing baseball with the Rocky Mount semi-pro team in North Carolina. The Olympic rules, since amended, stated very clearly that professional athletes could not compete. The International Olympic Committee ordered his name and records expunged from the rolls; he was required to send his medals back to Stockholm. Thorpe never really recovered from all this. Not much of a success as a baseball player, a football coach or a bit-player in the movies, he ended up living in a trailer near Lomita, California, where at the age of 64 he died of a heart attack.

Jesse Owens' was a happier story. Again, an astonishing athlete: The first time he ever ran a race in high school, his coach, Charlie Riley, thought his stopwatch was out of kilter. As a sophomore at Ohio State in May 1935, Owens broke three world records and equalled another in one afternoon. A few days before, he had fallen down some stairs and wrenched his back, which hurt so much on the day of the race that, as he recalled, "at both ends of that meet others had to help me get dressed and undressed."

For Owens' Olympics in 1936, the place to be was the vast Third Reich Sports Field in Berlin, capacity 110,000, to watch him win four gold medals in what he later referred to as "the most marvelous moment of my life."

Hitler was in his box when Owens ran the final of the 100 meters. The runners, six of them, went off in a bunch at the starter's gun. About 30 yards down the track Owens straightened and seemed to draw away effortlessly. He broke the tape a yard ahead of his teammate, Ralph Metcalfe. Despite the huge crowd's support of a German runner in the race, they gave Owens a rousing cheer for his effort. "Oh'vens! Oh'vens!"

Much has been made of whether Hitler snubbed Owens by not inviting him to his box, but it's hard to imagine that this was of much concern — there was a greater disappointment after his triumphs in the Games. Four Olympic medals turned out not to merit the Sullivan Award, given annually to the best amateur athlete in the U.S. It went instead to the decathlon champion, Glenn Morris. Not long after, entrepreneurs had Owens running exhibitions against racehorses. But he seemed to keep his humor about such exploitations. I always liked his explanation of how to beat a high-strung thoroughbred: Have the starter fire off his pistol so close to the horse's ear that it took a while for the jockey to settle him down. "By that time I was 50 yards down the track."

Jim Thorpe putting the shot in the 1912 decathlon. His performance was so strong in these Games that by modern scoring standards he would have earned a silver medal in the 1948 decathlon.

Jesse Owens is congratulated by a defeated Swedish sprinter after his 100-meter victory in Berlin.

Stella Walsh (no. 368, above) winning the 100 meters in 1932.

Babe Didriksen (right) on her way to a victory in the 80-meter hurdles in 1932.

A THIRD GREAT AMERICAN ATHLETE BEFORE THE WAR was Babe "Don't-Call-Me-Mildred" Didriksen, the sensation of the 1932 Los Angeles Games. From 1930-32 she held American, Olympic or world records in five different track and field events. One headline about her read "Babe Breaks Records Easier Than Dishes." She wasn't as large as one might expect from such a power athlete — 5'6½" and 126 pounds — but she was an all-American basketball player. She could punt a football 75 yards. She not only struck out Joe DiMaggio once, but also threw a baseball 313 feet. She rode (she was a Texan) and could hit a ball half the length of a polo field. And, of course, she became a legendary golfing champion (the first time she ever tried hitting a golf ball — according to Grantland Rice — it went 250 yards), winning a total of 82 tournaments.

Not only was she overwhelming at sports; she was also a renowned ballroom and adagio dancer, a whiz at backgammon, and could play the harmonica well enough to make a living at it. Paul Gallico, sportswriter for the *New York Daily News*, once asked her if there was anything she didn't play. "Yeah," she said. "Dolls."

The event I would like to have seen in Los Angeles was the javelin throw. She knew very little about the technique of throwing the thing. She threw it flat, like a catcher pegging a throw to second, rather than in an arc. On her first throw of the three allowed in the competition, the javelin never went higher than 10 feet, but nevertheless came within about 10 feet of the world record. She tore a tendon doing this, but the injury wasn't a factor because her competitors, in their successive tosses, never got closer than six inches to her mark.

How things have changed — techniques, training methods. These days, the German javelin thrower Petra Meier-Felke holds the world record at 262'5" — almost 120 feet farther than Babe's throw in those '32 Games.

Still, for her time the Babe was *non pareil*. The only woman even vaguely in her class was Stella Walsh, born Stanislawa Walasiewicz, the 100-meter sprint champion in 1932 from Poland. Years later, an innocent bystander, she was killed in a robbery attempt. An autopsy disclosed that although she had lived her life as a woman, she was in fact biologically a man.

Cassius Clay advances in the 1960 Games by defeating Shatkov of the Soviet Union.

I'D LIKE TO HAVE SEEN THE START OF MUHAMMAD ALI'S career in the 1960 Olympics in Rome, largely because he went on from there to become the most famous athlete in the world. He was 18 years old then, a light heavyweight, shy around girls, ingenuous and enormously popular in the Olympic Village, where one of his teammates remembered him for introducing himself to everyone, learning their names, exchanging lapel pins. "You would have thought he was running for mayor."

Known then, of course, as Cassius Clay, he won his first three fights in the 178-pound division, and in the finals faced a three-time European champion and future bronze medalist, Poland's Zbigniew Pietrzykowski. In the first round of the three-rounder, the American, confused by his opponent's unorthodox style, was badly mauled, and it took coming through in tremendous style in the third round — he had Pietrzykowski dazed on the ropes — to win the judges' votes and the gold medal.

There was one absolutely unpredictable outcome of his return to Louisville, his hometown, after his triumph in Rome. Across the street from his parents' house lived the Williams family, whose daughter, Lonnie, 5½, came out to see what all the excitement was about when the Olympic champion came home. Clay spotted her, and typical of his charm with children, picked her up, held her aloft, nuzzled her and said that he was going to marry her one day. He got on her tricycle, his knees pumping up about his chin, and raced her friends around the block. He recited some of his poems to her, one of which began:

> *To make America the greatest is my goal,*
> *So I beat the Russian, and I beat the Pole,*
> *And for the USA won the Medal of Gold.*

Twenty-four years and three ill-suited marriages later, he married Lonnie Williams. A graduate student from UCLA, with a strong clinical psychology background, and quite unlike his tempestuous former wives, she has proved to be an essential stabilizing factor in the boxer's extraordinary career that began in the 1960 Olympics.

In these same Games, I would like to have been present at the women's 100-meter butterfly race, when the 14-year-old American prodigy, Carolyn Wood, suddenly stopped swimming, having become disoriented after swallowing too much water. I wouldn't have enjoyed seeing *that* especially, but rather the moment when a fully clothed spectator, fearing she had suffered a serious cramp, flung himself into the pool to rescue her.

NOTHING IS MORE SATISFACTORY IN THE ENJOYMENT of games of skill than to have a complete unknown come from nowhere and win. The Olympics have had many such instances — perhaps none more memorable than Billy Mills's triumph at the 1964 Tokyo Games in the 10,000 meters, the only American ever to win at that distance.

A half-Sioux Indian, born in South Dakota, Mills was orphaned at 12. After a not particularly distinguished track career at the University of Kansas, he went into the Marines, where he was commissioned a lieutenant. He made the 1964 Olympics team largely because of the lack of competition at that distance in this country: He was given no chance at all in Tokyo. In fact, the day before the race, he had gone to a store in the Olympic Village, where a manufacturer was handing out free track shoes to the star runners. Mills was told that he did not qualify as a star performer and would have to pay for his shoes. The reporters ignored him, as did Australian Ron Clarke, one of the favored runners. Asked after the race if he had been worried about Billy Mills, Clarke replied, "Worried about him? I never heard about him!" No one had. After he won by three yards, improving upon his previous best time by 46 seconds, a Japanese official asked Mills at the finish line, "Who are you?"

A good explanation for feats of this sort was once offered by an American steeplechaser named Horace Ashenfelter, who unexpectedly won at his distance: "Olympic competition is so inspiring, and representing your country produces so much unexpected patriotism," he said, "that some athletes are moved to do more than they thought possible."

Dick Fosbury of the U.S. unveils his innovative "Fosbury Flop" in the 1968 Games.

UPI/Bettmann

I WOULDN'T HAVE MISSED THE MEXICO CITY OLYMPICS in 1968. That was when the high-jumper Dick Fosbury introduced the "flop," taking off and twisting his body so that, contrary to the usual route, he went over the bar backwards and head first, landing on his shoulders in the pit. "It's the only way I know how," he once said. "It's meditation — the idea in my mind of falling over the bar. The 'flop?' I don't care what they call it as long as it gets me over the bar."

Mexico City was also the scene of the famous protest of the two black U.S. 200-meter runners, Tommie Smith and John Carlos, who raised black-gloved fists and stood in black socks on the victory stand to protest symbolically racial inequality in their home country. Their act may have contributed to the most astonishing physical accomplishment of the Games, indeed what for twenty-three years has been called one of the most amazing athletic feats in history: Bob Beamon's long jump, soaring to a record which stood until recently. Beamon had opposed Smith's and Carlos's protest, but was enraged when the International Olympic Committee, headed by Avery Brundage, urged that the two athletes be punished. (They were subsequently suspended and sent home by the USOC.) In his first attempt in the Olympic finals, Beamon launched himself down the runway with a vengeance and jumped 29'2½", bettering the world mark, which had only increased 8½ inches since 1935, by an incredible 21¾ inches. A colleague of mine at *Sports Illustrated* found a felicitous phrase to describe this: Beamon had "leapt into the next century."

Bob Beamon lands his miraculous long jump of 29'2½" in Mexico City.

UPI/Bettmann

I talked to Beamon some months after and asked him what was going through his mind at the time of the jump. He said that he had hopped out of the jumping pit aware that he had made a fine jump, but nothing that he felt was truly out of the ordinary. He looked across the infield grass at the scoreboard, where the distances were marked in meters rather than feet and inches. Because the metric system was new to him, he wasn't instantly aware of his achievement. When Beamon finally realized what he had done, he practically lost consciousness, collapsing to the ground. He had to be helped to his feet by his teammates, dizzy and in tears.

GIVEN THE CHOICE BETWEEN WATCHING THE GYMNASTS Olga Korbut of the Soviet Union in the Munich Games of 1972 or the Romanian Nadia Comaneci four years later in Montreal, most people, I suspect, would opt to see the latter, the 14-year-old sprite who brought perfection to the sport with the first 10s ever recorded in the Olympics uneven bars and balance beam.

But in a way, Olga Korbut's was the more dramatic turn. In her white-ribboned pigtails she appeared in the Olympic *Sporthalle* in Munich as an elf-like figure (the "Elf from Grodno"),

Olga Korbut displays the championship form in Munich which brought her three gold medals and the world's adulation.

In 1976, Romania's Nadia Comaneci earned the first tens ever awarded in the Olympics on the balance beam and uneven bars.

weighing 85 pounds, with no signs of puberty, though she was, in fact, 17 years old. One forgets she was originally a substitute; she would not have performed were it not for an injury to a teammate. A Hollywood scriptwriter could not have done better. An unknown, Korbut came on the scene and her routines simply electrified, even frightened those more conditioned to the traditional emphasis on grace and purity. Some of her moves — back somersaults off the beam and uneven bars — seemed so reckless that several of the authorities wanted the routines banned. But the public was delighted. She became the star of the Games.

When she made several mistakes, which cost her a chance at the all-around title, she couldn't contain her disappointment: She hid her face in her hands and wept. This was seen by 400 million people on satellite television: It has been said that her tears were the most famous ever in sport. She still won three golds — in floor exercise, balance beam and team competition — and, more important, left a legacy. What an impact! Within a decade the number of women gymnasts in the U.S. would jump from 15,000 to 150,000!

I WAS IN LOS ANGELES FOR THE GAMES IN 1984. I remember best the great preponderance of flags — German, Union Jacks, Australian, French, even the spectators themselves decked out in flag patterns — their halters, briefs, jeans, spangled and striped. At the women's volleyball match, a group supporting the Chinese sat together. They carried little square flags of red silk. When their team scored a point the flags rose as one, a sudden shivering patch of color amidst the spectators, just there momentarily before coming back down smartly to their bearers' laps.

The athletes themselves were part of it. After winning the 100 meters in 9.99, Carl Lewis ran a victory lap with an American flag he had grabbed out of the stands, so large that he had to hold it above his head to keep its folds from dragging in the dirt of the track. The American 100-meter relay team almost disappeared under a huge Stars and Stripes provided them.

Having just won the 100 meters in 1984, Carl Lewis hoists the U.S. flag above his head.

Indeed, at the moment of victory the first impulse seemed to be to look for a flag. A country, however small, always seemed to have one available in the front seats of the Coliseum. When Said Aouita won the 5,000 meters, he reached into the stands and, like a conjurer, suddenly produced an enormous flag from his home — Morocco — a lovely vermillion with a five-pointed star in the middle. The largest I saw at the Games was one carried into the closing ceremonies by the Australians, who clustered around the edges while bringing it in horizontally. It was so large that they were able to flip a girl, wearing a knapsack for some reason, high in the air as if she were being bounced at the shore on a giant beach blanket.

Of course, there were other vignettes that I would not forget, that would remain like freeze-frames when I thought about that Olympics: the women's 3,000 meters and the tangle between Mary Decker and Zola Budd, the little, barefoot runner formerly from South Africa (what one sportswriter referred to as the most famous collision since the *Titanic* met the iceberg), and how Decker tore off Budd's number from her back as she fell and began weeping in frustration on the infield grass.

Certainly I would remember the sturdy pertness of Mary Lou Retton, arms aloft on her landing from the vaulting horse, having scored a perfect 10 with the double-twisting Tsukahara, and then doing another just for the glory of it, pounding down the runway as if to show she was incapable of a fluke.

I would remember how the crowd quieted down when Greg Louganis moved to the edge of the 10-meter platform for the last dive of the Olympics — a reverse 3½ tuck, the so-called Dive of Death that had killed Sergei Shalibashivili the year before, when the Soviet diver hit his head as he spun back towards the platform — and the great roar that went up when Louganis scored an unheard-of 10 from one judge to finish with the highest total (710 points) ever scored in platform diving competition.

Joan Benoit celebrates after winning the first women's marathon in 1984.

I would remember Joan Benoit winning the women's marathon, the first time the event was run in the Olympics. She ran a victory lap carrying an American flag. Her time, 2:24:52, would have won 13 of the 22 *men's* Olympic marathons.

And finally the closing ceremonies themselves, with the magnificent A Touch of Class, the horse that won the show jumping gold, circling the track with two other equestrian medalists.

But always the flags. There was a brisk trade in them at the vendors' stands as the crowd filed out of the Coliseum. On that last day what everyone wanted was the Olympic flag with its five interlocking rings....

Greg Louganis, the only man to win both the platform and springboard titles in two Olympics.

CHAMPIONS
EIGHT LEGENDARY OLYMPIANS

BY BRIAN CAZENEUVE

From the moment the first medal was awarded in 1896, the Olympics have been universally recognized as defining the standard of athletic excellence. The champions it produces every four years are justly acknowledged as the world's best in their individual events. To celebrate the 1992 Games — and the athletes who compete in them — we have chosen to tell the stories of eight distinguished gold medalists. Unique in their accomplishments, at the same time they represent the ideals that the Olympics have always sought to embody. The skill, courage and character they demonstrated on the way to their gold medals are the same qualities which will be on view at Barcelona. In honoring these eight from around the globe, we honor the spirit of the Olympics and all those, winners as well as losers, who participate in the Games.

◆

Brian Cazeneuve, special Olympic correspondent for Time *magazine in 1988, has covered sports for* The New York Times, Washington Post *and* Associated Press, *among others. He writes regularly for* The Olympian *magazine.*

Crowds flock to the first modern Olympics at Athens in 1896.

Emil Zatopek

It hurt to watch Emil Zatopek run. He moved with mouth agape, teeth crunched and eyes closed. His stride broke down into flailing knees and elbows devoid of form and visible purpose, and his rattling head appeared ready to spin off his neck at any moment.

It also hurt to run against Emil Zatopek. He relied not on pace but on irreverent mid-race dashes that exhausted muscles and shattered wills. He picked strategic points — uphills, downhills, sharp curves — places where others hoped to catch their breaths, to make his moves. He won a silver and a gold medal in the 5,000 and 10,000 meters respectively in the 1948 London Olympics, and made history in Helsinki four years later, sweeping the 5,000, 10,000 and the marathon, a feat unlikely to be duplicated.

Always the innovator and experimenter, he trained at times with a gas mask to control his breathing and with combat boots to strengthen his legs. He carried others on his back. He ran upstairs, in his bathtub, in place, anywhere. To perfect his legendary finishing kick, he developed the now common practice of interval training: shorter, faster, gut-wrenching sprints within an unyielding workout of distance and endurance.

"It was thought that in improving the muscles that go fast," he explains, "you compromise muscles that go far. But to be a champion, you must tell overworked muscles to work hardest when they are weakest."

Together with his wife, Dana, a champion javelin thrower whom he married after the 1948 Olympics, he went to the 1952 Helsinki Games hoping for an unprecedented family double. Emil was the first Zatopek to win — at 10,000 meters, and four days later at 5,000 meters as well.

After the second awards ceremony, Dana rushed to him, tossed his medal into her warm-up bag for good luck and went out to throw. She won the competition with her first effort. "The score of the contest in the Zatopek family is 2-1," Emil reminisced afterwards, "too close. To restore some family prestige, I will try to improve on it in the marathon."

The only problem with this idea was that Emil had never run a marathon before, and didn't have any particular sense of how you go about winning one. He decided his best hope was to stay near Briton Jim Peters, the experienced favorite. Peters set out in a fast pace in an effort to lose Zatopek, but after 10 miles the two were together. Inquiring if the pace were fast enough, Zatopek was told by a wearying Peters that it was too slow, at which point Emil sped up and raced past him. Peters dropped out at the 20-mile mark.

With the stadium in sight, Zatopek was struggling. Or was he? As usual, his limbs swung with little semblance of sync, and he seemed to run each step of the last mile on hot coals. It also happened to be his fastest of the entire race. With his face contorted by grimaces, he wobbled across the finish line, the only man ever to win all three Olympic long-distance races.

"I was not really a good runner," he insists. "No technique, no style. And I was so tired that day. But fatigue is like pain. You either give up or fight with more intensity. Little pain is a problem. Big pain is no problem. The pain must be great enough to get you through the pain barrier so you stop for nothing."

Zatopek's pain barrier would be tested after retirement, too. Outspoken in his support of Czech reforms in 1968, Emil was silenced when the Russians moved in, forbidden to travel or to speak publicly. The country's greatest athletic hero was banished to toil in uranium mines. It was not until the Havel government that he and Dana were fully rehabilitated. Today, they grow and sell vegetables in Prague.

Yet Emil remains surprisingly unbitter, grateful instead for the marvelous memories and the warm friendships of fellow competitors. "Linked in this sporting combat," he says, "is the friendship between adversaries — deeper than that with your neighbor who shares only your neighborhood. Your rival, you understand him."

On and off the track, Emil Zatopek ran and lived with passion. "I made many friends," Zatopek says. "Only to those who tried to change me or saw me run was I the *enfant terrible*."

Fanny Blankers-Koen

It's 3 p.m. and Fanny Blankers-Koen is at her best. She's worried.

"I hope I have enough to say. Sorry the house is not so clean. Please excuse my English."

From her neatly kept, second-story Amsterdam apartment, Blankers-Koen, 73, speaks with great clarity about life in the fast-paced city which cannot keep up with her.

"These days I am like this," she says, placing a chair in her path and pushing her way around it. "Excuse me, Sir, I must hurry. My friend waits. I have a lot to do and not much time." She never waited very long for anything — except perhaps her Olympic victories.

Francina Koen was only 18 when she competed in the 1936 Games in Berlin. She won no medals, but remembered fondly the chance to travel, the big stadium and the joy of getting an autograph from Jesse Owens, the man whose four-gold performance she would later equal.

It was her dream to return to the Olympics, but it was not until 1948, after the war had cancelled two Games, that she was able to realize it. By then she was a 30-year-old mother of two — hardly an auspicious candidate for gold medals. "At that time, athletes did not make favorable women; mothers did not make good athletes. Also, the English papers said, 'Fanny is 30, too old.'"

But the newspapers did not understand Fanny's need to win not just for herself but for others. "My husband was my coach," she says. "I had to make the finals for him. Then the other girls told me, 'Fanny, you must do well for us,' so I was like this," she demonstrates, clenching her fist. "I ran faster carrying the wishes of other people."

Running not to disappoint those who believed in her, she became the only female track athlete to win four gold medals in a single Olympics. She won the 100- and 200-meter sprints, the 80-meter hurdles and anchored Holland's 4x100-meter relay team to victory.

The world-record holder in the high jump and long jump, she would undoubtedly have won those, too, if her event schedule had permitted her to compete in them. Fanny, it turned out, was not too old.

Each event retains its own unique set of associations for her. After sloshing down a muddy track to win the 100 meters, she walked to the podium, anticipating the playing of the victory anthem. But she never heard it. "I was looking at the flag," she says, "and instead I saw my father dancing around the kitchen table. Our tune was over before I remembered it."

Her hurdles race was so close that both she and Britain's Maureen Gardiner suffered cut necks from hitting the finish string at the same time. When Blankers-Koen heard "God Save the Queen" she assumed she had lost, until she realized that British officials were simply acknowledging the presence of the King and Queen in the royal box.

By the time of the 200-meter final, she wanted to leave and return to her children, but was convinced by her husband to stay. As she describes her tension before the race, she suddenly kneels in a starting position and grabs at the carpet as if ready to bolt out of the living-room window. "I thought, maybe they'll fire the pistol and I won't know how to move."

She moved well enough to win by the enormous distance of seven meters, and well enough also to come from way behind in anchoring the relay. Receiving the baton in fourth place, "I thought it was not possible to win. But something, I don't know what it was, made me say, 'Come on. Push.' Before I knew it, it was over and I was first."

After the London Games she set another world record in the pentathlon. Following her retirement from active competition, she became a track administrator until just before her husband's death in 1977.

Blankers-Koen's extraordinary athletic gifts are matched by an extraordinary humility. When she recalls the tumultuous, city-wide celebration arranged for her upon her return to Amsterdam from London, she reveals the same modesty that characterized her as a champion: "I couldn't believe it — people, presents, flowers. I was so embarrassed because it was all only for me. I had hoped I had really done something special at these Games to make people care."

UPI/Bettmann Inset: Dimitri Georganas

Rafer Johnson

Rafer Johnson has traveled a great distance in his life — from the railroad station where he lived for a year with his family to the presidency of the UCLA student body, from the difficult economic circumstances of his youth to a friendship with America's most powerful family, the Kennedys. But perhaps his toughest journey was the 1,500 meters he had to survive to win the 1960 Olympic decathlon.

The 1,500 meters is the last and most debilitating of the decathlon's 10 events. Run at the end of two days of exhausting competition, it requires everything an athlete has to give. To know its pain is to know the decathlete.

"Nothing to it," winces Johnson. "In the previous 48 hours you haven't had time to eat a full meal. Every muscle hurts. If you haven't pulled, sprained or popped something, you think you're not trying. Forget about sleep. Understand, running 1,500 meters isn't tough at all; running it hard when your body's like soup is a torturing test of character."

In the Rome Olympics, Johnson's character met that test. He entered the 1,500 with a 67-point advantage over his UCLA teammate and friend, C.K. Yang, needing only to stay within 10 seconds of Yang to win the decathlon. (Decathlon scoring is computed on the basis of a weighted point scale for each event.) Yang's best time in the 1,500 was almost 18 seconds faster than Johnson's.

Under the lights (it was 9:15 in the evening), Yang set out to break Johnson's will and win by the necessary 10 seconds. The race's drama was made more poignant by the fact that the same man — Ducky Drake of UCLA — was coaching both athletes. Drake had advised each of the best strategy.

"He told me not to let C.K. get too far ahead, and then told C.K. where in the race he should try and lose me. 'Don't let him go with you,' he warned C.K.; 'Rafer, you have to go with him,' he urged me."

Both attempted to follow Drake's advice. Yang struggled to lose him; Johnson refused to be lost. As Yang strained to pull far ahead, he was implacably pursued by his friend and rival who finally crossed the finish line only 1.2 seconds behind him. Johnson had won the decathlon.

"I didn't know I had him until the last six or seven strides. And at the end I was too tired really to feel elated. I didn't have the strength to raise my arms or anything. C.K. didn't have the strength to congratulate me either, so we sort of leaned on each other, tried not to tip over."

Johnson's pursuit of Yang actually began shortly after the 1956 Melbourne Games, which he entered as a strong favorite to win the gold. But he began them with a damaged knee, ripped a stomach muscle warming up for the long jump and competed at half strength thereafter, hobbling finally to a silver medal.

"I was disappointed" Johnson remembers, "but I wasn't shaken, just really driven. The whole thing hammered home the fact that they don't give Olympic gold medals away. Sometimes you have to work harder than you think you'll have to in order to win one. If you don't, there are no excuses, only four more years of training if you want another chance."

Johnson's brilliant victory was by no means his greatest honor. As captain of the U.S. team at Rome, he was chosen to carry the American flag at the opening ceremonies, a task he found almost as challenging as finishing the 1,500. "It's funny," he says. "What did that flagpole weigh, 10 pounds? Fifteen pounds? But when you realize what an honor it is that you're carrying your country's flag, the thing is like a 100 pounds. You think, 'What if I trip? What if I get a cramp?'"

Johnson didn't stumble, any more than he stumbled when he was chosen to light the Olympic flame to open the 1984 Games at Los Angeles. He remembers the day he went up the stairs with the torch as clearly as any day in his life.

Johnson has not been selfish about his good fortune. Having previously started a big-brother/sister program for international university students and traveled throughout the world for the Peace Corps, he is currently director of the California Special Olympics, where he helps, as he says, "a segment of our society that not enough people realize has so much to share."

Rafer Johnson's grace has never been confined to his performance on the track.

Olga Korbut

Olga Korbut came to the gymnastics competition at the 1972 Munich Games with unabashed freshness. Off the beams, bars and mats she was every bit the impetuous 17-year-old, determined not to accept her assigned place in the inflexible Soviet gymnastics hierarchy. On them, Olga — she didn't need the last name — was a kid frolicking through the park. An Olga routine was a celebration of life, and when the Olympics were over, she left behind her standards of gymnastics which had been transformed by her imagination.

Olga came from the industrial Byelorussian city of Grodno, where she was initially rejected from gymnastics classes because she appeared too fragile. She persisted, however, and a local coach named Renald Knysh finally took her on when she was 9. "It was his mistake," Korbut says. "Many times I gave him a heart attack."

Olga often sneaked off after regular sessions to do something crazy on the uneven bars. "I was like a monkey trying to swing and learn by touch and feel. I didn't know how to do anything, but I needed to learn like I needed to breathe."

Knysh knew it, too. He'd see Korbut spill, cry and, without any urging, vigorously attack the apparatus which had just rebuffed her. Her extended hands could barely reach the balance beam, but this was an indefatigable tiger.

"My trainer was a forward-thinking man," she says. "If I told him, 'I want to fly this,' he wouldn't say, 'No, you must be wooden like the others.' He would say, 'You must let me show you the right way to prepare it.' It was a fair compromise. We trusted each other, and we were both bored by the old style of gymnastics."

Olga progressed through the Soviet national ranks in spite of the suspicion with which the traditionalists viewed her acrobatic risk taking and impishness. "Our judges and Olympic coaches didn't want me to do the difficult skills, to shine the light away from [defending world champion] Lyudmilla Turischeva. She was a proper Russian girl, so she was supposed to win. But that is a lie, not a competition. In competition, you do your best."

Knysh made sure she would by giving her instructions to memorize before she went to bed. "I would do each routine in my head 10 times as hard as I did in practice," she says. "It was like a story, a play for many people in the audience but no judges. My trainer told me, 'The people matter; the judges don't.' And in the Olympics, the people would finally be my judge."

In Munich, the 4'11", 85-pound giant would wow them all, including the judges. She landed an unheard of back flip on the beam, sailed through a back-diving chest roll on the floor and seemed to do the surreal on the bars. In one dream-like sequence, she stood on the top bar, flipped backwards in a full layout, recaught the bar, swung to the low bar and spun around it on her stomach, ending up catching the high bar, facing the opposite direction.

What's more she giggled. She skipped. She waved. Nobody ever waved. These were Soviets, as dour as they were dominating. Astonished, the world adopted Olga.

And when she stumbled — as she did when scraping the floor at the beginning of her uneven-bars routine — and dismounted in tears, she endeared herself even more. People loved an athlete who wasn't intent on hiding her emotions, of joy as well as sorrow. Although that error ended up costing her the all-around title, her gold medals for beam and floor exercise were applauded throughout the world.

Soon after the Games, Olga toured the United States, setting attendance records for gymnastics in every major city she visited. New York's Mayor Lindsay gave her the key to the city; Chicago's Mayor Daley declared an official Olga Korbut Day.

After winning a gold and silver at the '76 Montreal Games, Olga married and retired from competition to a coaching career. But her concern for people did not end with her departure from the gymnastics hall. Following the 1986 Chernobyl nuclear accident, which occurred near her Minsk home, Olga became active in raising funds to help diagnose and treat those who were exposed to excessive radiation. Through her efforts, vital equipment is being purchased and Soviet physicians trained to help treat patients with radiation-related illnesses.

"People from all over the world are helping," she says. "It doesn't matter where you are from if people are in your heart."

Al Oerter

Al Oerter's enthusiasm for the discus won't go away. Neither will he. Oerter, 55 going on something much younger, still trains and competes in Masters' events with the same joy and zest to achieve that earned him four Olympic gold medals between 1956 and 1968.

"The Olympic experience spoils you," he says. It alters not only your perception of track and field, but of life. If you can derive that much enjoyment and be that successful in something theoretically adversarial, then there isn't much you can't do."

Though the newness and wonderment may have vanished with his millionth spin-and-hurl, the feelings associated with the perfect delivery remain. For Oerter, it's the feeling that lifted his discs on their winning flights.

"Ever walk into an Olympic stadium with the greatest athletes from every corner of the globe compressed into that one confined area? You're there with people who have spent four years strenuously preparing to test themselves, in some cases, for as little as 10 seconds. That just heightens the sense that what you've worked for and thought about each day is actually here — that one day you've been preparing for."

In Oerter's four triumphant days, spaced over 12 years, he established himself as perhaps the greatest pressure competitor in Olympic history. Though he never won an Olympic trials and always faced a different world-record holder at each Olympics, Oerter, "too young," "too old," or "too injured," set a new Olympic record every time.

"I think I was proudest of never being the favorite, and perhaps subconsciously I set myself up for it, or at least was more comfortable with it," he says. "People, athletes especially, need the challenge that comes from having something to prove, not so much to other people as to themselves, which is why I enjoyed the sport so much. The day after the Games ended, I knew the next great challenge was four years away."

Oerter treated the pressure like a swirling, virulent wind which had an inevitable impact on every toss. If ridden properly, it could make the disc float; if ridden poorly, it could run the disc aground. One could almost picture him extending a wet finger to gauge the gust of nerves and ride whatever soar particles were milling around the discus ring.

"The reason I was able to do well under pressure," he says, "is that I was always able calmly to step outside myself and look from a distance at the adjustments I had to make. Most people look for an excuse to be distracted — they sneeze, their foot's asleep, the wind isn't perfect — but I tried to think harder about less: leg drive, arm placement, specifics. That way you respond better to the adversity that actually exists."

Oerter had plenty to respond to. Prior to winning the 1960 Rome Games, he survived a near-fatal car crash. After missing most of the 1963 season with a chronic cervical disc injury, he arrived at the 1964 Tokyo Olympics with a large harness around his neck. "People didn't expect me to do much," he remembers.

Oerter was able to ignore the pain in his back once he ripped some cartilage in his rib cage a week before the Games. It was presumed he would not compete, but instead he showed up with bandages, ice packs and the stubbornness to think he had one great throw in him. He figured it would have to be his first one.

Doubling over in pain after each release, however, Oerter was in third place after four of his six throws, and his attempts to hold form were becoming feeble. He rethought his approach and bent over to start his fifth throw in slow motion. Saving all the strain for the point of release, Oerter uncrumpled and made the first 200-foot throw in Olympic history.

For Oerter, "The best way to overcome pain is to get lost in the euphoria of your best performance. You can only do it once, though. I had no throws left at that point."

Soon after the 1968 Mexico City Olympics Oerter retired, history's only four-time champion in an individual track and field event. Now a corporate spokesman, he has no plans to stop throwing the discus. Why should he? "Something like that," he tells himself after uncoiling on a field near his Florida home. "Feels good."

Dawn Fraser

Long before she became the first woman freestyler to swim 100 meters in under one minute, Dawn Fraser was already making waves. At 14, after defeating Lorraine Crapp, her highly regarded teenage rival, she was suspended for two years by the Australian League of Swimmers. Her club, it ruled, had spent too much money on her trophy.

"I don't know if it was a witch hunt or a misunderstanding," she says, "but it was not a pleasant experience at 14 to hear people accusing me of being a professional swimmer."

Despite her precocious talent, Fraser was considering a career as a dressmaker when a coach named Harry Gallagner convinced her to leave her family in Sydney and come to Adelaide to train with him. Swimming in an unheated pool in an unheated building during Adelaide winters tended to be difficult. "I remember after a hard sprint, getting out of the pool with headaches, frozen ears and white hands and I'd think, 'This is nuts.' But I always wanted to go back in. You get caught up in the challenge."

Fraser kept going back and in 1956 qualified for the Melbourne Games. "It was my first Olympic Games in front of all those people. It was almost impossible to sleep: I dreamed I got halfway down the pool and couldn't finish. It was like I was in a bowl of spaghetti and I couldn't get out."

Fortunately there was water in the pool, not pasta, and Fraser swam swiftly through it to win, just barely defeating teammate Crapp.

Once certain she had won, Fraser headed for the stands to share the moment with her parents. "The media people had some seats in front of the stands where my mom and dad were sitting. So I walked on their tables, which was actually out of bounds for the swimmers. Sometimes you bend the rules a little," she says.

After defending her title at the Rome Olympics in 1960, and breaking the one-minute barrier two years later, she looked forward enthusiastically to the '64 Tokyo Games. Seven months before them, however, her world collapsed: A car she was driving slid into a truck. She suffered a non-paralytic broken neck; her mother was killed.

Fraser assumed her career was over. "I had lost my best pal. What did I want with swimming? But then my teammates came around the house and told me they wanted me back. Slowly I knew that was what I needed."

No one knew what to expect of her at the Tokyo Games, but she soon revealed that all was well when she defied what she took to be a foolish team order forbidding swimmers from marching in the opening ceremonies: "Hey, these swimmers have trained all their lives for a chance to be here, and you tell me they're not fit enough to march?" Fraser asks. "This is the whole spirit of the Olympics. That's why you swim in freezing water — to be here."

Fraser also had a problem with an uncomfortable team swimsuit. After discovering that local tailors couldn't fix it, she had a new suit made in roughly the same team colors, and with a team patch. No one seemed to notice except the Australian officials, who warned her that she would be disciplined for her behavior.

They waited until after the Games when "Granny," as she was known to her admiring teammates, had won another gold. Then the Australian Swimming Federation suspended her for 10 years (later reduced to four) for shunning the suit and joining the ceremony.

"I think some people had been waiting to get me ever since they first heard of me — the brash girl from the wrong neighborhood. But I wasn't ever going to change or stop speaking my mind."

Nor did she. Her uncompromising honesty got her elected to Parliament in 1988, and her Olympic achievements (four gold and four silver medals) resulted in her being named Australia's greatest female Olympian and the first athlete inducted into her country's Hall of Fame.

Her reverence for the Olympics is as unassailable as her fierce independence. "I had a chance to go back to Greece recently and see the ancient arenas at Olympia. It was mind-boggling to be able to sit on the stone where the torch was first lit. It shook me. I don't think anything else in my life shook me. But the Olympics do that to you. That's what they're all about."

Bill Bradley

For all his time on the basketball court, Senator Bill Bradley's most noteworthy tip-off may have occurred during a post-game interview when he referred to his N.Y. Knicks teammates as constituents. He gave a subtle indication then that he might one day run for something other than a loose ball and defend his position on a floor not made of hardwood.

As an all-American at Princeton and a 10-year starter with the Knicks, Bradley was always thinking ahead, trying to make his opponents guess. Would he shoot or pass? Go left or right?

"Unconventional choices catch people off guard. That can help a basketball player or even an elected official," he says, smiling. "But wanting to take part in the Olympic Games was probably the easiest decision I could have made. Ever since I could remember, I wanted to be in the Olympics. I certainly wasn't the world's greatest athlete, but I was lucky enough to become a pretty good basketball player."

He never tired of studying the game. While he admired it as "a great metaphor for larger societal cooperation," he also loved it for what he calls its "beautiful isolation — the back-door play that works, the daring pass, the ripple of the net that quiets a hostile crowd. I played for these moments."

In August 1964, while still a Princeton student, he arrived at the Olympic training camp on a military base at Pearl Harbor, where coach Hank Iba set out to mold an assortment of individual stars into a cohesive team. He did it by turning the 20-day camp into basic training. "We practiced in a sunken gym that was about 100 degrees," Bradley recalls. "The Iba workouts lasted three hours in the morning and three more in the evening. After the morning session, we'd all wring out our sneakers — not our socks, our sneakers, which never dried in time. Iba made us into a team by reducing each man to the same level of exhaustion."

Because the 1964 team did not have the offensive power of its predecessor, Iba stressed defense — dog-him, double-team-him, wear-his-jersey defense. "We ate and slept that word," Bradley says.

As a result, U.S. opponents shot a frigid 29 percent from the floor and averaged twice as many turnovers as the Americans. Bradley, the complete player, was the only man in the top three of every U.S. offensive team statistic.

Overcoming second-half deficits against Yugoslavia and Puerto Rico, the U.S. advanced to the finals to play the Soviets. Bradley had come prepared. He had memorized some handy phrases while studying Russian history at Princeton. Roughly fouled minutes into the game, he startled the culprit by shouting "Watch out, big fella," in Russian.

"Until then, the Soviets had called their plays verbally," he says, "but after that they stopped talking to each other. They started cutting in the wrong direction and throwing errant passes."

The U.S. won, leaving Bradley with his fondest memory: the awards ceremony. "It's a very patriotic feeling naturally, hearing your anthem, seeing your flag. It seems too short at the time, but it lasts forever."

Bradley was also struck by the difference between the opening and closing ceremonies. "In the opening, you marched in an orderly way with your country. But in the closing, the athletes marched in together, talking with friends they had made from different nations. I walked in with an athlete from Nigeria, two from Poland, an Italian and some Australians. Even though the basketball games are sort of a blur, I clearly remember trading T-shirts, learning foreign phrases and walking around the Olympic Village."

Bradley, who received a Rhodes Scholarship after leaving Princeton, sees his basketball career with the New York Knicks and his election to the Senate as extensions of his Olympic experience. "In my life I always wanted to meet different types of people, attempt a different challenge. On the road, I tried to answer fan mail and see the city I was in rather than sit in a hotel. I think the Olympics were my first chance to do all these things at once."

When asked how a quiet, essentially private person chose to become a public figure, Senator Bradley also finds the answer in the Olympics. "Taking part, isn't that what Baron de Coubertin said about life and the Olympics? That's what I'm doing."

UPI/Bettmann Inset: Alan Dorow

Alberto Juantorena

Alberto Juantorena remembers his greatest childhood wish when growing up in Cuba. "I wanted to run," he says, cycling his feet and pumping his fists. "I could never take many hours in a day without a large, open place calling my name."

Today, Juantorena still finds those open places with voices to call him. Only now they are voices of children, living their own childhood wish — to run along with "El Caballo," "The Horse," as Juantorena is called. Perhaps the greatest sports hero in a country which reveres sporting achievement, he remains a man who still just wants to run.

"I jog to stay in shape," says Juantorena, who at the 1976 Montreal Games became the only man in Olympic history to win both the 400 and 800 meters. "I don't move fast."

Although he also played baseball and basketball as a boy in the seaport city of Santiago de Cuba, where he was born, he moved fast enough to be admitted, at 19, to the Havana Institute for Physical Culture, where his training as a runner began. While there was much to learn about the skills of running, young Alberto relished the immediate gratification of it: "When you run, time doesn't matter. If you run well, of course, you will have a fast time. But you run the best when you run for the feeling of running fast, when today doesn't care what you do tomorrow, when the ground is telling you, 'go, go, go.'"

In his first year at the institute he ran a 51-second 400 meters in tennis shoes while institute officials debated whether to spend money on spikes for him. When finally allotted spikes, he ran 48.20 by the year's end, and several months later was selected to represent Cuba at the 1972 Munich Olympics. He missed a berth in the 400 finals by one place.

Determined to do better at the next Games, he was nevertheless slowed by various injuries to his left foot in 1974 and 1975. But this hardly mattered to Zigmundt Zabierzowski, Juantorena's Polish coach, who nurtured the private vision that his pupil could win not only the 400, but also the 800 at the Montreal Games.

Juantorena had run the 800 only three times prior to the Games. Each race, Zabierzowski told him, was merely a longer interval run to increase his stamina for the 400. "He prepared me in secret so as not to arouse my suspicions that he was crazy," Juantorena explains. "Only two weeks before Montreal he told me I will run both. At first I was like a volcano on the worst day — big, big explosion. I was a fast car, not used to conserving the gas. But my coach understood my ability."

After two unspectacular qualifying heats in the 800, Juantorena began the race that would astound the experts. Most thought he would hang back in the pack and try to use his sprinter's speed for a surge at the finish. Instead, he bolted for the front at 600 meters, and by the time U.S. favorite Rick Wohlhuter realized what was happening, there was no stopping him. Juantorena's nine-foot-long stride continued to open ground, and he crossed the finish line in 1:43.50, setting a new world record. "Maybe being mad helps you run faster," he laughs.

Four nights later, he completed his extraordinary double, this time pulling the 400-meter race out in the last 50 meters. Of his performance in the final, Juantorena comments, "The first 380 meters came from the legs. The last 20 came from the soul."

In all, Juantorena ran nine races in nine days, losing 11 pounds in the process. In response to a question about his exhaustion, he replies, "What is fatigue? It is the tiger saying he doesn't want his prey. It is resignation, not physical injury. It is like an injury of the mind. I am going to have this at the Olympic Games? My friend, please...."

Injuries prevented him from matching his achievements in the following Olympics, but he had already become a legend. Now one of Cuba's highest-ranking sports officials, he is also the most beloved. He still partakes in the country's "People's Marathons," 10-kilometer jogs through the streets and parks that turn Havana Sundays into family holidays. His times are slowed, he says, because so many people want to shake his hand during the run.

"This is the spirit of the run," he says, talking with his hands as much as in words, "to fight in the spirit of play."

ATHLETICS - TRACK

By James Dunaway

MEN
100m
200m
400m
4 x 100m Relay
4 x 400m Relay
110m Hurdles
400m Hurdles
3,000m Steeplechase
800m
1,500m
5,000m
10,000m
Marathon
20km Walk
50km Walk

WOMEN
100m
200m
400m
4 x 100m Relay
4 x 400m Relay
100m Hurdles
400m Hurdles
800m
1,500m
3,000m
10,000m
Marathon
10km Walk

SPRINTS

Speed is a part of every running event, even the marathon (there isn't a runner alive who doesn't want to run faster).

But there is a special drama about the explosive muscles, and explosive egos, of sprinters. At every Olympics, the first moment of total silence in the track stadium comes late in the second day of competition, when eight finalists in the men's 100 meters hunch into their blocks at the starting line.

The sprinter risks all for a moment of glory. If he wins, he is king of the world, at least for the moment. If he loses, even by an inch, he is — again, for the moment — nothing.

Perhaps you remember the scene in Seoul after Ben Johnson had beaten Carl Lewis in the 100-meter finals. Lewis could hardly bear to look at Johnson as he offered a perfunctory handshake to the Canadian. In that moment, even Carl Lewis, arguably the greatest track and field athlete of all time, felt the crushing ignominy of the losing sprinter.

To be sure, Lewis shook it off quickly. After all, he had to get ready to defend his long jump championship the next day. And, of course, three days later he was declared the 100-meter winner after Johnson was disqualified for using steroids. But Lewis never enjoyed that unforgettable instant of victory; in fact, he was handed the 100-meter gold medal in an office under the stadium instead of on the winner's stand.

Johnson's lackluster performances upon returning to competition in 1991 after a two-year suspension seemed to prove conclusively that he cannot run with world-class sprinters without steroids; he appears to have almost no chance of making the 100 finals in Barcelona. But don't automatically concede a third straight gold medal to Lewis. His training partner, Leroy Burrell, who took away Lewis's 100-meter world record in 1991 with a 9.90-second performance and then finished a close second in 9.88 as Lewis regained the world record with a 9.86 victory at the World Championships in Tokyo, won't let their close friendship prevent him from trying to win in Barcelona. And remember that four others — Dennis Mitchell of the U.S., Linford Christie of Britain, Ray Stewart of Jamaica and Frank Fredericks of Namibia — all finished within a meter of Lewis in that world-record race.

In any case, 1992 will almost certainly conclude the 31-year-old Lewis's remarkable Olympic career. He is not only the first athlete ever to win two Olympic 100-meter gold medals and two long jump gold medals, but his total of six golds in four events

Winner of bronze medals in the 1984 Olympic 100- and 200-meter races, Jamaica's Merlene Ottey would like to prove to herself that she can earn the gold.

Carl Lewis

Track & Field News named him Athlete of the Decade in 1989, but many feel he is the greatest track and field athlete of all time. At 30, starting a new decade at the 1991 World Championships in Tokyo, Lewis set a world record in the 100 meters (9.86 seconds), a world record in the 4x100-meter relay (37.50), and turned in the four best long jumps of his life (it took a world record by Mike Powell to beat him and end his 65-meet, 10-year winning streak). In short, Carl Lewis is improving with age. What keeps him going? "Carl loves to compete," says Tom Tellez, his coach since he was 18. "And the tougher the competition, the better he likes it." Barcelona will probably be Lewis's farewell to Olympic competition; win or lose, he's worth watching every time he steps onto the track.

---

is the most by any track and field athlete since Paavo Nurmi's nine between 1920 and 1928. It will be interesting to see if King Carl can add two or three more in Barcelona.

Watch lanes 3-6 in the sprint finals, where the fastest runners start.

Johnson will occupy a less happy place in history. But the drug test he failed two days after the 100-meter final in Seoul turned out positive in more ways than one. It forced the International Amateur Athletic Federation to adopt a serious program for stamping out drug use in track and field. Today, athletes can be tested for drugs year round, not only during competition, but while training as well.

As a result, you can expect that more than one world-record holder will be missing at Barcelona because of drug infractions. In the sprints, Harry "Butch" Reynolds, the American 400-meter world-record holder, failed a steroid test late in 1990 and probably won't be eligible to compete.

But there's still plenty of quality in the longer sprints — the 200 and 400 meters. Lewis, the 200 winner in 1984 and 1988 runner-up to his Santa Monica Track Club teammate, Joe DeLoach, may return, as well as the 1988 third and fourth placers, Robson da Silva of Brazil and Christie. To them, add Burrell, Fredericks and 1990 European champion John Regis of Britain. In the 400, despite the likely absence of Reynolds, the excellent field still includes the other two Americans at Seoul, gold and bronze medalists Steve Lewis and Danny Everett; 1991 world champion Antonio Pettigrew of the U.S. and runner-up Roger Black of Great Britain; and Roberto Hernandez of Cuba, the world's best non-American 400 runner since 1988. He has the extra incentive of having missed the Seoul Olympics when Cuba boycotted the Games in sympathy with North Korea.

Looming larger than all of them at 200 and 400 meters is 24-year-old Texan Michael Johnson. Prior to 1990, Johnson was known as a talented but oft-injured runner — a hamstring pull in 1987, a stress fracture in '88, another hamstring in '89. But in 1990, Johnson finally stayed in one piece and

---

James Dunaway, author of Sports Illustrated Track and Field: Running Events, *has covered track and field for the Associated Press,* The New York Times *and numerous other publications.*

It might only be a scheduling conflict that could prevent Michael Johnson of the U.S. from winning both the 200 and 400.

put together the greatest combined 200-400 season in track history, and then tacked on an even better one in 1991. Even such a great as Tommie Smith never managed to be ranked No.1 in the world in both events in the same year; Johnson did it two years in a row.

The biggest obstacle between Johnson and a 200-400 double may be the Olympic timetable, which requires eight races in five days. Johnson hopes to make the U.S. team in both events, then decide whether to run just one or both in Barcelona.

Dramatic as the men's sprints were in Seoul, a woman — Florence Griffith Joyner — stole the show from Carl Lewis, Ben Johnson and Co. by winning three gold medals and one silver medal.

Will another FloJo emerge at Barcelona?

There are three likely candidates: 22-year-old Katrin Krabbe of Germany, the 1991 world champion at 100 and 200 meters; 27-year-old Gwen Torrence of the United States, who finished second to Krabbe in both races at Tokyo less than a year after having a baby; and 32-year-old Merlene Ottey of Jamaica, who was favored to win both, but had to settle instead for two bronzes.

Torrence should be much improved in 1992, with the added strength of an extra year of training and the added confidence of barely missing two gold medals. Ottey, although she had the year's fastest times in 1990 and 1991 at both the 100 and 200 meters, must now face doubts about her ability to run at the top of her form in major races.

But the favorite has to be Krabbe. Not only did the former East German win both World Championship races, but she is also carrying on a strong tradition. From 1972 through 1988, East and West German women won more than half of the sprint medals available to them — and if it hadn't been for Griffith Joyner in 1988, the percentage would have been higher.

In the 400 meters, another former East German, 20-year-old Grit Breuer, will meet tough competition from world champion Marie-José Perec of France; 1988 Olympic champion Olga Bryzgina of the C.I.S.; and Cuba's brilliant Ana Quirot, who because of boycotts has had to sit out the last two Olympics.

In a race with six runners breaking 10 seconds, Carl Lewis set a world record of 9.86 in the Tokyo 100-meter finals.

Carl Lewis, Andre Cason, Dennis Mitchell and Leroy Burrell joined forces in Tokyo and walked off with a new 4x100 world record.

Katrin Krabbe

Nobody's life has changed more dramatically in the last two years than Katrin Krabbe's. She grew up in the gray, disciplined East German sports system: At 13, she left home to enter a sports school, where she trained twice a day with other promising teens, closely supervised by professional coaches. When she wasn't training, she studied to be a kindergarten teacher. In 1988, at 18, she set a world junior record in the 100 meters. Nine months after the Berlin Wall came down, she won the European 100- and 200-meter titles, and BANG! — she was the most famous woman in Germany. Flashbulbs everywhere, modeling jobs, magazine covers and a Mercedes didn't make her lose her focus. She kept on training and became an even better sprinter, winning the 1991 World Championship 100 and 200 convincingly. In Barcelona, she will be tough to beat.

RELAYS

Relay running sometimes looks like it's just a matter of the four fastest runners winning the race, but it isn't that simple. It takes precise baton passing, as well as sheer speed, especially in the 4x100-meter relay, where the difference between a good pass and a so-so one can be a loss of three meters. For a perfect pass, the outgoing runner must match his or her speed perfectly to that of the incoming runner, and the exchange must be made with both runners' arms fully extended — all within the passing zone. That requires plenty of practice, not just in workouts, but in actual races as well.

The United States, which on paper should have won every men's Olympic relay in history by a comfortable margin, has in fact lost several of them. In 1988 at Seoul, the U.S. men's 4x100 team was disqualified in the first round for an out-of-the-zone pass and never even got to the finals. The American women eliminated themselves from the World Championship 4x100 relay at Tokyo when they dropped the baton.

Why does the United States, which almost always has the fastest sprinters, have so much trouble with the Olympic relays? The answer lies, in part at least, in the way the team is selected. Most nations, with only a few good sprinters, choose their national relay teams as much as two years in advance of the Olympics, which gives them plenty of time to perfect their baton exchanges.

The American team isn't chosen until after the U.S. Olympic Trials, usually no more than two months before the Games. In addition to having very little time to practice together, the top American sprinters have often been more interested in winning medals in the individual sprints than in preparing for the relay. When they do work together, as the 1991 American men's 4x100 team did when it set a world record in Tokyo, the results can be stunning.

But never forget, it's not the four fastest runners, but the fastest *team* that wins.

Billy Konchellah failed to make the talented Kenyan team for the 1988 Games, but returned to form and won the 800 meters at the 1991 World Championships.

Middle-distance runners have to choose: they can try to lead all or most of the way, or follow for most of the race and try to win with a sprint finish at the end. A runner who lacks a strong finishing kick has little choice; he or she has to stay at or near the front, and at some point must take the lead and try to build up such a large margin that the kickers can't overcome it.

(The very best runners — Jim Ryun or Said Aouita in their primes — are so talented in sheer running ability that they can win with any tactics. But if a group of runners is fairly evenly matched, as is generally the case in the Olympics, the best *racer* usually wins.)

Being a front runner has many advantages. You can decide how the race will be run: how fast the pace will be, or how slow. You escape the bumping and shoving that goes on in middle-distance races. And you can stay close to the curb and avoid running wide. Running in the second lane adds an

extra three to four meters per turn. Running in lane two all the way in a 1,500-meter race adds at least 20 meters to the distance. If you run 1,520 meters in a 1,500-meter race, you have to run three seconds faster to beat the runner who runs just 1,500 meters; that's too much for even the greatest runner.

But it's lonely out there in front, and many runners feel more comfortable staying close to the lead instead of in it. Not only is there less wind resistance (just as in cycling), but there's also a better view of what's going on in the race. So you'll often see almost everybody trying to occupy the same space, just behind the leader. That's one reason why there is so much physical contact — major pushing and shoving — in the 800 and 1,500.

It isn't only the men who race rough. Women middle-distance runners can be just as tough. For example, look at Suzy Favor Hamilton. At 5'3½" and 105 pounds she looks frail and helpless — but she was neither when she shouldered and elbowed her way past PattiSue Plumer on the inside to win the 1991 U.S. national 1,500-meter title.

PattiSue Plumer of the U.S. (left) came from behind to beat Great Britain's Liz McColgan in this 5,000-meter race in 1989. Plumer will be a strong medal contender in the 3,000 at Barcelona.

One thing you'll almost certainly see in the men's middle-distance and distance races at Barcelona will be the continuing dominance of the Africans — not only from East African nations such as Kenya, Tanzania, Somalia and Ethiopia, but also increasingly from Morocco and Algeria in North Africa.

In the 1988 Games, Kenyan men won four of the five distance races on the track, and the fifth was won by a North African. African runners also won a silver and two bronze medals to give them eight out of a possible 15 medals.

Last year in Tokyo, four *different* Kenyans won four of the five distance races on the track, with the fifth being won by a North African; this time, Africans won 12 of the 15 distance medals, and only one was a repeater from Seoul.

The depth of their distance-running strength is what is really startling about the Kenyans. When Paul Ereng won the 800-meter gold medal in Seoul, he was a virtual unknown in international competition. Since then, he has gone on to win two world indoor championships and set a world indoor record. But in the 1990 world rankings of *Track & Field News*, Ereng was only the fourth-ranked Kenyan 800-meter man, behind William Tanui, Nixon Kiprotich and Stephen Ole Marai. And Billy Konchellah, the 1987 800-meter world champion, who didn't make the Kenyan team for Seoul, came back to win the 1991 World Championship.

In other words, before Kenya's four 1988 Olympic champions can defend their titles in Barcelona, they'll have a tough time winning a place on the team in their Olympic trials a month or so before the Games start. Just for the record, besides Ereng those 1988 gold medalists are Peter Rono in the 1,500 meters, John Ngugi in the 5,000 meters and Julius Kariuki in the 3,000-meter steeplechase. The 1991 world champions are Konchellah, Yobes Ondieki in the 5,000, Moses Tanui in the 10,000 and Moses Kiptanui in the steeplechase.

North African distance running came into its own at the the 1984 Olympics when Moroccan Said Aouita crushed the field to win the 5,000-meter gold medal. Four years later, Aouita took the bronze medal in the 800 meters at Seoul, running on a hamstring so sore he could barely walk an hour before the race. But an Aouita protégé, Brahim Boutaib, won the 10,000 meters easily with the fourth-fastest time ever run, 27:21.46.

World Records (as of 1/12/92)

Event	Men				Women			
100m	9.86	C. Lewis	USA	1991	10.49	F. Griffith Joyner	USA	1988
200m	19.72	P. Mennea	ITA	1979	21.34*	F. Griffith Joyner	USA	1988
400m	43.29	B. Reynolds	USA	1988	47.60	M. Koch	GDR	1985
800m	1:41.73	S. Coe	GBR	1981	1:53.28	J. Kratochvilova	TCH	1983
1500m	3:29.46	S. Aouita	MAR	1985	3:52.47	T. Kazankina	URS	1980
3000m					8:22.62	T. Kazankina	URS	1984
5000m	12:58.39	S. Aouita	MAR	1987				
10,000m	27:08.23	A. Barrios	MEX	1989	30:13.74	I. Kristiansen	NOR	1986
4x100m relay	37.50	Cason, Burrell, Mitchell, Lewis	USA	1991	41.37	Moeller, Rieger, Auerswald, Goehr	GDR	1985
4x400m relay	2:56.16*	Matthews, James, Freeman, Evans / Everett, Lewis, Robinzine, Reynolds	USA / USA	1968 / 1988	3:15.17*	Ledovskaya, Nazarova, Pinigina, Bryzgina	URS	1988
100m hurdles					12.21	Y. Donkova	BUL	1988
110m hurdles	12.92	R. Kingdom	USA	1989				
400m hurdles	47.02	E. Moses	USA	1983	52.94	M. Stepanova	URS	1986
Steeplechase	8:05.35	P. Koech	KEN	1989				
Marathon■	2:06:50	B. Densimo	ETH	1988	2:21:06	I. Kristiansen	NOR	1985
10 km walk■					41:30	K. Saxby	AUS	1988
20 km walk■	1:18:13	P. Blazek	TCH	1990				
50 km walk■	3:37:41	A. Perlov	URS	1989				

*World record set at Olympics   ■World best, not world record

Steeplechase world champion Moses Kiptanui's toughest competition might well come from his own teammates at Kenya's Olympic qualifying trials.

Chuck Muhlstock

Noureddine Morceli

In 1989, a promising 19-year-old runner left Algeria to study and train at Riverside Community College in southern California. There, coach Ted Banks introduced him to a training regimen more intense than he had ever seen, including plenty of speed work to go with his natural stamina. It worked: By the end of 1991, he was unbeaten in 15 races at the mile and 1,500 meters, including both the indoor and outdoor World Championships. His average margin of victory — against the world's best runners — was more than 10 meters. Part of his strength is his confidence; as one of his friends says, "When Morceli goes to the starting line, he believes he will win."

Aouita, who holds the world records for 1,500, 2,000, 3,000 and 5,000 meters, underwent surgery on both legs in 1990, and his recovery to gold-medal form is uncertain. But in the meantime, he and Boutaib have been joined at the top of world-class distance running by a number of others, most notably Khalid Skah, winner of the 1990 and 1991 World Cross Country individual championship, perhaps the single toughest race in the world.

The latest North African sensation is not a Moroccan; he's a young Algerian named Noureddine Morceli. Morceli zoomed from 49th-fastest 1,500-meter runner in the world in 1989 to first in 1990, and proved it wasn't a fluke by setting the 1,500-meter indoor world record in 1991. Morceli, like Aouita, is a great runner *and* a great racer. If we're lucky, we may see them facing each other in the 1,500 final in Barcelona.

We know we'll be seeing Kenyans and North Africans in the distance races, even if we don't know who will be running and at what distances. Some others to look for are: 800 — George Kersh and Mark Everett of the United States, Tom McKean of Great Britain and 1991 world silver-medalist Jose-Luiz Barbosa of Brazil; 1,500 — redheaded Peter Elliott of Great Britain, the (British) Commonwealth Games champion, and Simon Doyle of Australia; 3,000-meter steeplechase — European champion Francesco Panetta of Italy; 5,000 and 10,000 — Salvatore Antibo of Italy, who won both European titles, and Arturo Barrios of Mexico, world-record holder at 10,000 meters, who is almost as good at 5,000.

The women's distance races appear to be wide open. At 800 meters, Cuba's Quirot will face Germans Sigrun Grau-Wodars and Christine Wachtel, 1-2 in Seoul. A comer to watch is 19-year-old Maria Mutola of Mozambique, who at 18 finished fourth in the World Championships, just four feet away from the gold medal. The two top runners in the 1,500 should be world champion Hassiba Boulmerka, a fast-finishing 24-year-old Algerian, and 29-year-old Natalya Artyomova of the C.I.S.

The time schedule offers intriguing possibilities for doubling in the 3,000 meters and either the 1,500 or the 10,000. American PattiSue Plumer has a chance for a medal at both 1,500 and 3,000 meters. So does the C.I.S.'s Tatiana Dorovskikh, who as Tatiana Samolenko finished first in the 1988 Olympic 3,000 and third in the 1,500, and then at the 1991 World Championships, a year after becoming a mother, won the 3,000 and took second in the 1,500. She'll be even tougher in Barcelona. In the 10,000, Lynn Jennings of the United States will be one of the favorites, along with world champion Liz McColgan of Great Britain, Kathrin Ullrich of Germany and Yelena Romanova of the C.I.S. And if she can stay healthy, Mary Decker Slaney of the U.S. might finally win a medal at any one of the three distances.

MARATHON

The Olympic marathon is never the biggest marathon of the year, and it is hardly ever the fastest. But it is always the most important, and it usually provides the best television coverage.

Today's London, New York City and Berlin marathons, with some 25,000 entrants each, are in sharp contrast to the Olympic fields: 100-150 in the men's race and 100 or less in the women's.

But although the fields are small, the quality is extremely high. Both 1988 Olympic champions — Gelindo Bordin of Italy and Rosa Mota of Portugal — have stayed at or near the top of the rankings since Seoul and can be expected to defend their titles. Bordin will have his hands full, fighting off a host of talented African runners, including Seoul runner-up Douglas Wakiihuri, a Kenyan who lives and trains in Japan. Mota will probably face her strongest opposition from world champion Wanda Panfil of Poland.

Poland's Wanda Panfil capped another great year on the roads with the 1991 World Championship marathon title.

WALKS

Race walking is a somewhat arcane discipline, with two major rules: (1) the walker must remain in contact with the ground at all times, which means the leading foot must hit the ground before the rear foot leaves it, and (2) the leg in contact with the

ground must be straightened at every step. To put it in a nutshell, the walker must go fast, but not too fast.

Like the marathon, the walks start and finish in the stadium, with most of the course outside on the roads. But instead of one long loop or out-and-back course, walkers go around and around a loop usually of 2,000-3,000 meters.

The reason? So the judges can keep a close eye on the form of the walkers and make sure they don't "lift" (lose contact with the ground) or "run" (fail to straighten the knees). A walker is disqualified when violations are called by three different judges.

At Barcelona, women walkers will compete in the Olympics for the first time. They'll compete over 10,000 meters, compared to the two men's events of 20,000 and 50,000 meters.

Holder of Mexico's first track world record (in the 10,000 meters), Arturo Barrios (foreground) is stirring up distance racing's established order.

ATHLETICS - FIELD

By James Dunaway

MEN
High Jump
Pole Vault
Long Jump
Triple Jump
Shot Put
Discus
Javelin
Hammer
Decathlon

WOMEN
High Jump
Long Jump
Shot Put
Discus
Javelin
Heptathlon

JUMPS

The key to successful jumping is not what takes place in the air, but what happens before the jumper leaves the ground.

That's because the "jump" in all four events is a combination of as much speed as the jumper can control and a takeoff which provides as much straight-up lift as the jumper can muster.

All jumpers measure the length of their run-ups carefully before the competition, making adjustments for the speed of the takeoff surface and the wind. If necessary, they keep adjusting during the competition: If the position at the takeoff isn't right, the jump won't be either. Tom Tellez, who coaches Carl Lewis, once wrote, "90 percent of coaching should be done on the run and takeoff." He was writing about the high jump, but it applies almost equally to all the jumps.

During the 90 seconds allowed for each jump (two minutes for the pole vault), you may notice that many jumpers seem to be just standing at the head of the runway. Are they waiting for the wind to change? Frequently they are. But they're also rehearsing the perfect jump mentally, picturing each step of the run-up, the takeoff, the action in the air and the landing: reminding themselves, in short, of what they have to do, and focusing all their energies on doing it.

◆ HIGH JUMP ◆

When Dick Fosbury of the U.S. won the 1968 Olympic high jump in Mexico City, his "Fosbury Flop" was the sensation of the Games. Hardly anyone had ever seen a high jumper fly over the bar backwards before.

Today, it's unusual to see a high jumper who *doesn't* use the flop technique. In fact, all jumpers at the 1988 Games, men as well as women, were "floppers."

But the best men's high jumper in the world in 1988 wasn't at the Seoul Olympics because of the Cuban boycott. Javier Sotomayor could not compete, despite setting a world record of 7'11½" (2.43m) just two weeks before the Games began. A year later, "Soto" became the first jumper in history to clear eight feet.

In Barcelona, he'll finally get a chance to win the gold medal he might have won four years earlier. His toughest competition should include Sweden's Patrik Sjoberg and Americans Charles Austin — who won the 1991 World Championship

Mike Powell / Allsport

Gerard Vandystadt / Allsport

Mike Powell / Alls

after Sotomayor withdrew with an injury — and Hollis Conway.

In the women's high jump, world-record holder Stefka Kostadinova of Bulgaria should be the co-favorite with 1991 world champion Heike Henkel of Germany.

One of the great innovations television has brought to track and field is the point-of-view (POV) camera, which puts the viewer's eye close up and right along the top of the high jump and pole vault crossbars as the jumper goes over. It gives you, the viewer, a unique opportunity to see what actually happens during the attempted clearance.

◆ POLE VAULT ◆

Perhaps the strongest favorite in any 1992 Olympic event is Sergei Bubka of the C.I.S. Not just because he has raised the indoor and outdoor world records more than 25 times, not just because he was the first to clear 20 feet (6.10m), but simply because he has won most of the major competitions he has entered since winning the 1983 World Championship as an unknown. If anyone is to beat Bubka, now 28, the most likely candidate is 23-year-old Istvan Bagyula of Hungary, a former student at George Mason University in Virginia, who finished a surprise second to Bubka in the '91 Worlds.

When you watch the Olympic pole vault, think about this: The vaulter must run at top speed while carrying a flexible 12-pound, 17-foot pole and then plant the end of the pole into a six-inch-wide box set in the runway. And he has to do it *automatically*, so he can concentrate on the hard part — clearing the crossbar 18 or 19 feet overhead.

The pole vaulter's strategy is similar to the high jumper's: Take as few jumps as possible at lower heights to conserve energy for the 19-feet-and-up jumps, where Olympic medals are won. At Seoul, Soviets Bubka and Rodion Gataullin, who finished 1-2, didn't start jumping until the bar was at 18'8¼" (5.70m), a height cleared by only four other vaulters in the competition.

◆ LONG JUMP ◆

The long jump has produced the two most famous American Olympic athletes of recent years: Carl Lewis and Jackie Joyner-Kersee. Although Lewis has won gold medals in the sprints, and Joyner-Kersee is the world-record holder and Olympic champion in the heptathlon, both began as long jumpers.

Anatomy of a new world record: (from left) Mike Powell breaks Bob Beamon's 23-year-old long jump record by two inches; expresses his immediate joy; watches anxiously as rival Carl Lewis tries to eclipse his mark; collapses in ecstasy as he realizes he has won; and celebrates with a young admirer.

rd Vandystadt / Allsport

Mike Powell / Allsport

Stefka Kostadinova

From 1985 through March 1989, the willowy Bulgarian high jumper raised the world high jump record three times, losing only seven times in 103 competitions. But one of those seven losses was in the 1988 Olympics, where she initially tied for first with American Louise Ritter, only to lose in a jump-off for the gold medal. In the spring of '89, Kostadinova broke what a Bulgarian journalist described as "the little finger of her left foot," missed four months of training, and decided to take a year off from jumping and get married. She still had her mind on the high jump, though — the train of her wedding gown measured 2.09 meters (6' 10¼"), exactly equal to her world record. Her return to competition in 1991 wasn't exactly a barn-burner (sixth in the World Championships), but another year of hard training should see her, at 27, ready to win the gold medal this time.

When Mike Powell long jumped 29' 4½" (8.95m) to win the World Championship last August 30, he gained almost as much fame for ending Lewis's 10-year winning streak as for breaking Bob Beamon's 23-year-old world record. He also set up expectations for an exciting rematch in Barcelona.

Powell's next goal is nine meters (29'6½"), and of course he hopes to trade up the silver medal he won four years ago in Seoul for a gold one in Barcelona. But don't expect Lewis to go quietly. He jumped well enough in Tokyo to win every other long jump competition in history, and he still must be considered at least co-favorite with Powell.

After all, Lewis has won two Olympic titles and has exceeded 28 feet twice as often as all other jumpers combined.

One reason he is so hard to beat is his absolute confidence in his run-up. His takeoff foot is usually within two inches of the foul line, jump after jump after jump. When the POV camera is focused on the long jump takeoff board, watch how consistent Lewis's takeoffs are compared to those of the other jumpers.

The women's long jump was one of the competitive treats of the 1988 Games. The lead changed six times before Jackie Joyner-Kersee finally emerged the winner over Heike Drechsler of Germany and Galina Chistyakova of the U.S.S.R. Each has held the world record (most recently Chistyakova), and their Barcelona meeting should be just as dazzling as it was in Seoul.

◆ **TRIPLE JUMP** ◆

The triple jump is perhaps both the most beautiful and physically demanding event in track and field. Every component of the track and field athlete's repertoire is called for: speed, power, flexibility, balance, technique, stamina and concentration; weakness in any one of them is almost always fatal to high-level performance.

Dan O' Brien

As a senior (class of '84) at Henley High in Klamath Falls, Oregon, Dan O'Brien won four state track championships as well as all-state honors in football and basketball. A seeming natural for the decathlon, O'Brien had a disappointing career at the University of Idaho — too much partying, too many academic eligibility problems, too many injuries. Finally coach Mike Keller told him: "Get your act together, or get out!" So O'Brien buckled down, and things began happening. In 1990, he emerged "suddenly" to take second in the U.S. championships and the Goodwill Games; in 1991, he posted two of the top five decathlon scores in history and won the World Championship with an American record. At 6'2½" (1.90m), 185 pounds (84kg), he's perfectly built for a decathlete. He's also still improving; in 1991, he scored personal bests in seven of the decathlon's 10 events and just missed in the other three. Bruce Jenner, move over.

The event used to be called the hop, step and jump, which is an accurate description of its three parts. But in practice the three parts must be blended into one continuous, flowing effort. That's what makes it so enjoyable to watch, and so difficult to master at the world level.

Kenny Harrison and Mike Conley of the U.S. should be strong medal contenders — they finished 1-3 at the Tokyo World Championships — but with 14 of the top 15 jumpers of all time still competing, chances are that the medals will be won by whoever gets hot on the day of the finals. One worth watching is Leonid Voloshin of the C.I.S., who took the silver medal at Tokyo in only his second year of triple jumping.

THROWING EVENTS

Comparisons of meets over the last 10 years show that performances in the throwing events have fallen off significantly. Athletes just aren't achieving the distances with the discus and shot that they formerly did. Obviously, something has changed, at least as far as shot put and discus efforts go. Many experts agree that the change is for the better — the consequence of diminished use of steroids and other performance-enhancing drugs brought about by more rigorous monitoring programs.

In the future, results in the shot put and discus may continue to lag behind those of the early 1980s, both because of more stringent drug testing as well as the disintegration of the regimented Eastern Bloc sports system, which produced some of the world's leading athletes in the throwing events.

◆ SHOT PUT ◆

After shot putter Randy Barnes of the United States set a world record of 75'10¼" in May 1990, he became a favorite to add a gold medal in Barcelona to the silver he won in Seoul. But later that year, Barnes tested positive for steroids and was suspended for two years; his chances of winning an appeal seem slim.

Sergei Bubka

Before he took up pole vaulting, Sergei Bubka of Ukraine was a soccer player. Once, in 1980, Bubka's pole vault coach wondered aloud if he shouldn't go back to playing soccer; three years later he won the World Championship. Bubka went on to raise the world record 28 times (13 outdoors, 15 indoors) between 1984 and 1991. He's at his best with his back to the wall: He won the gold medal in the 1988 Olympics with a last-chance clearance of 19'4¼" (5.90m), and did it again in the 1991 World Championships at 19'6¼" (5.95m) despite an injury. Even before the economic transformation of the Soviet Union, he became a capitalist, earning an estimated $1 million per year (at least) from appearance money, world-record bonuses and a shoe contract. Has it made him soft? No way, says Bubka: "I want to set more records."

At Seoul, Ulf Timmermann of East Germany, then 25, won the gold medal with a last-round put of 73'8¾" (22.47m) to overtake Barnes's 73'5½" (22.39m). With Barnes almost certainly out of the competition, it looks as if only 1988 bronze-medalist Werner Günthor of Switzerland stands between Timmermann and another gold medal. Günthor showed how much he has improved by easily winning the 1991 World Championship (Timmermann was out with an injury), so their Barcelona showdown should be exciting to watch.

You'll see two styles of shot putting in the Games. One is the familiar "glide" style perfected by two-time gold-medal winner Parry O'Brien of the U.S. in the 1950s, in which the athlete drives straight across the seven-foot ring from back to front. The other is the "spin," or discus style, originated in the 1960s, in which the thrower makes one and a half full turns in the ring before launching the shot.

The two techniques seem to be equally effective in producing long throws, and which one a thrower uses is a matter of personal preference.

In the women's shot, world-record holder and 1988 Olympic champion Natalya Lisovskaya of the former U.S.S.R. will face her strongest challenge from China's Huang Zhihong, who upset Lisovskaya in the World Championships.

◆ **DISCUS THROW** ◆

Before the first modern Olympics, the discus throw had not been contested since the ancient Olympic Games ended in 393 A.D. The Greeks actually reinvented it for the 1896 Games to give them some of the flavor of the past.

Robert Garrett of the United States and Princeton University made up his mind to try the

Event	Men				Women			
High jump	8'0"	J. Sotomayor	CUB	1989	6'10¼"	S. Kostadinova	BUL	1987
Pole vault	20'0"	S. Bubka	URS	1991				
Long jump	29'4½"	M. Powell	USA	1991	24'8¼"	G. Chistyakova	URS	1988
Triple jump	58"11½"	W. Banks	USA	1985				
Shot put	75'10¼"	R. Barnes	USA	1990	74'3"	N. Lisovskaya	URS	1987
Discus	243'0"	J. Schult	GDR	1986	252'0"	G. Reinsch	GDR	1988
Hammer	284'7"	Y. Syedikh	URS	1986				
Javelin	293'11"	S. Backley	GBR	1990	262'5"	P. Meier-Felke	GDR	1988
Decathlon	8847 pts.*	D. Thompson	GBR	1984				
Heptathlon					7291 pts.*	J. Joyner-Kersee	USA	1988

*World record set at Olympics

event (making the Olympic team was a simple matter in those days: you decided to go) and practiced with a homemade steel "discus" created by a friend. When he arrived in Athens, Garrett was delighted to find that the real discus was much lighter and easier to throw. He went on to defeat the stunned Greeks, who had anticipated winning the event without any trouble.

Garrett's winning throw measured 95' 7½" (29.15m), a distance which would not win many junior high school meets today. Incidentally, he also won the shot put and finished second in the long jump and third in the high jump.

Three of the top throwers in the 1992 discus competition are former East Germans, and each has a legitimate shot at the gold medal. Wolfgang Schmidt, 38, held the world record from 1978-81; Jürgen Schult, 32, is the defending Olympic champion and world-record holder; Lars Riedel, 25, won the 1991 World Championship in Tokyo. Schmidt, banished from competition by his own East German federation between 1981 and 1987 for being politically outspoken, rebuilt his career after moving to West Germany; Schult blossomed to become East Germany's No.1 during Schmidt's absence. Now they as well as Riedel compete for a united Germany, and it's quite possible they'll be the last three standing in the battle for the gold medal at Barcelona. Two Americans, veteran Mike Buncic, 30, and young Kamy Keshmiri, 23, are also strong contenders in the wide-open field. Lithuania, competing again as an independent nation, has two strong candidates for the gold: Romas Ubartas and Vaclavas Kidikas.

The former East German women discus throwers, including Seoul winner Martina Hellmann, should continue their rivalry with the C.I.S., led by Larisa Mikhalchenko. But the favorite should be 23-year-old Ilke Wyludda of Germany, who has been almost unbeatable since 1989 despite competing regularly against the best throwers in the world. Tsvetanka Khristova of Bulgaria upset Wyludda with a last-round throw in the World Championships, but Wyludda is the most consistent thrower in history.

◆ HAMMER THROW ◆

The hammer ranks with the pole vault and triple jump as the most difficult track and field events. The 16-pound ball is connected to a three-foot, 10-inch wire with a triangular handle. Gripping the handle, a thrower accelerates by spinning three

It was no surprise that javelin world-record holder Petra Meier-Felke of Germany won the gold at Seoul, as she has won nearly 90 percent of her events since 1984.

Olympic discus silver medalist in 1976 for East Germany, Wolfgang Schmidt was later banned and imprisoned for his outspoken desire to live in the West. Competing now for a unified Germany, Schmidt would love, at 38, to win another Olympic medal.

49

World champion Yuri Syedikh heads a powerful C.I.S. hammer squad that swept all the medals in the last two Olympics in which the U.S.S.R. participated.

or four times at ever-increasing speed within a seven-foot circle before letting it go. Done properly, it flies 260 feet or more; if not, well, there's always another time.

The throwers who do it best come from the former Soviet Union. In the last four Olympics in which they competed (i.e. not including 1984), Soviet hammer throwers won 11 of the 12 medals awarded. The triumvirate which swept the medals for the U.S.S.R. in 1980 and 1988 — Yuri Syedikh, Sergei Litvinov and Yuri Tamm — are all in their mid-30s now, and they're being pressed by a new generation of throwers, led by Igor Astapkovich and Andrei Abduvaliyev. With 12 or more of the world's top 20 in most years coming from the old U.S.S.R., winning a spot on the Commonwealth team can be tougher than winning an Olympic medal.

◆ JAVELIN THROW ◆

It's hard to know *what* to expect in the men's javelin. In the mid-1980s, when throws started to exceed 100 meters (328'), the International Amateur Athletic Federation (IAAF) rewrote the specifications for the javelin to bring distances back under 90 meters (295'). For a while it worked, but then javelin designers found ways to put new aerody-

Upset in the 1991 World Championships, Natalya Lisovskaya from the former U.S.S.R. hopes to regain her world-record form in time to win a second Olympic gold in the shot put.

namics into the spear (within the rules), so that recently Seppo Raty of Finland improved the world record to 96.96 meters (318'1"). Now the IAAF has rewritten the rules again, and the "modified" new javelins won't be allowed in the 1992 Olympics. In the process, Raty's record was erased and replaced by the 293'11" mark achieved with the traditional javelin by Great Britain's Steve Backley in 1990.

Raty is still the world's best thrower, although he was edged out by his fellow Finn, Kimmo Kinnunen, in the World Championships. Others who could earn medals include Backley, Jan Zelezny of Czechoslovakia and Patrik Boden of Sweden. Along with Raty, these three competitors have taken turns raising the world record in the past two years.

Despite a stunning upset in the women's javelin at the World Championships by Xu Demei of China, three former East Germans could dominate at Barcelona. Besides Petra Meier-Felke, 33, the world-record holder and defending Olympic champion, who has won nearly 90 percent of her competitions since 1984, Germany has two superior younger throwers in Karen Forkel, 21, and Silke Renk, 25.

One interesting challenger is Norway's Trine Solberg Hattestad; she was suspended for steroids

Jackie Joyner-Kersee

When she fell to the track in Tokyo last August with a hamstring pull, Jackie Joyner-Kersee had won 14 heptathlons in a row since losing by five points in the 1984 Olympics. Within minutes, Bobby Kersee, her husband and coach, was putting a positive spin on the injury. "This will keep Jackie motivated for Barcelona," he said, as if she needs motivation. At 30, Jackie is the same fierce competitor on the track, the same smiling, easygoing person off the track she has always been. She still makes regular visits to the ghetto neighborhood in East St. Louis where she grew up and now supports a youth center like the one that helped her as a teenager. At Barcelona, she'll try to defend the long jump and heptathlon gold medals she won in Seoul. "She's looking for perfection," says Bobby, "and she's willing to pull every muscle in her body to achieve it."

in 1989, but in 1990 became the first person ever to win a reversal from the IAAF Doping Commission. After having a baby later that year, she roared back impressively in 1991. She's still angry about the suspension — perhaps that could be all the motivation she needs in Barcelona.

MULTI-EVENTS

Traditionally, the winner of the Olympic decathlon is known as "the world's greatest athlete." In 1992, an American will be favored to win it for the first time since Bruce Jenner was expected to (and did) in 1976 at the Montreal Games.

In the World Championships in Tokyo last year, Dan O'Brien won by a wide margin with 8,812 points, the fifth-highest score ever, despite mediocre performances in the high jump and discus. Unless O'Brien is injured or makes a major mistake, the rest of the field in Barcelona will be competing for silver and bronze. They include American Dave Johnson, the favorite until O'Brien came along; the 1980 and 1984 Olympic champion, Britain's Daley Thompson; 1988 gold-medalist Christian Schenk of (East) Germany; France's Christian Plaziat, the 1990 European champion; and Canadian Mike Smith, the (British) Commonwealth Games champion.

Everybody knows who the "world's greatest *woman* athlete" is: the 1988 Olympic heptathlon champion, Jackie Joyner-Kersee. Her two days of glory in Seoul, where she won the gold medal with her fourth world record in a little over two years, planted dreams in as many young heads as Olga Korbut did for gymnastics in 1972. In the years B.J. (Before Jackie), when a coach asked an athlete to try the heptathlon, the reaction more often than not was, "What's a heptathlon?" These days it's, "You mean like Jackie?"

Joyner-Kersee competed sparingly in 1989 and 1990, but she's building up to another maximum effort for Barcelona. In addition to endorsements and public appearances, she has also been working on sharpening her skills in her three weakest events, the shot put, the javelin throw and the 800 meters.

There doesn't really seem to be anyone likely to come along and knock her off the top step of the victory stand in Barcelona. Her nearest competitor, European champion Sabine Braun of Germany, who won the World Championship when Joyner-Kersee dropped out with an injury, is hundreds of points behind.

BASEBALL

By Vic Ziegel

MEN'S EVENT

Centerfielder Jeff Hammonds of Stanford University is perhaps the best all-around talent on the U.S. team.

The U.S. has a long and glorious history in Olympic baseball. The key word here is history.

Baseball has finally become an Olympic medal sport at the Barcelona Games, eight teams swinging aluminum bats in search of the gold. Baseball, as we all know, is thoroughly American. Nobody is certain where Mudville is, but there's no doubt Casey was an all-American strikeout. The first game, at least the first score, was a 23-1 romp in 1846 in Hoboken, New Jersey. The first professional baseball team, Cincinnati's Red Stockings, opened shop in 1876. The World Series began in 1903 in Boston. There was only one Babe Ruth and he was one of ours. The Bronx Bombers and The Hitless Wonders and The Gashouse Gang and The Boys of Summer and The Whiz Kids were all American success stories.

Although the game was born here, and grew up here, it has traveled well. The International Baseball Association, the world governing body, now has 71 member nations, each one with a Hank Aaron and Sandy Koufax of its own.

The U.S. is not the favorite in this newest Olympic medal sport. Cuba is the country most likely to bring back the first baseball gold. We are next, or maybe after next, behind the Japanese, who beat

Vic Ziegel, columnist for the New York Daily News, *recently published* Sunday Punch, *a collection of his sports pieces.*

the U.S. in the demonstration final of the 1984 Games in Los Angeles — a U.S. team, no less, with future professional stars Will Clark and Mark McGwire. Japan and the U.S. were in the finals four years later, and this time, ah, this time, Jim Abbott, now with the Angels, pitched the U.S. to victory.

Cuba, boycotting, stayed away from both of those Olympics. Last summer, in the Pan Am Games, the U.S. lost to Cuba, the eventual gold-medal winner, 3-2, and Puerto Rico, silver winners, 7-1. We came away with a bronze, barely, outlasting the Dominican Republic, 2-1, in 15 innings.

Those four Pan Am finalists have qualified for the Olympics along with Spain, the host country; Italy, winner of the European Championships; and Japan and Taiwan, the top two teams in the Asian Championships.

If U.S. prospects in the present are uncertain, the past is firmly American. Baseball's first Olympic appearance was in the 1904 St. Louis Games, with two U.S. teams playing each other. In 1912, the Americans went to Stockholm and soundly trounced a Swedish squad to whom they had lent a pitcher. Olympic baseball wasn't seen again until 1936 in Berlin, when the one game was between two American teams. The sport was back on hold until 1952 in Helsinki, when American athletes in the Olympic Village put together a ball team and beat Finland, 19-1. U.S. military personnel serving in the Far East were flown to the Melbourne Olympics in 1956 and crushed the host nation, 11-5. The 1964 U.S. team took care of Japan, 6-2, in Tokyo.

There will be no Roger Clemens or Darryl Strawberry playing for the U.S. at Barcelona. Unlike hockey and basketball, professionals cannot compete in Olympic baseball, so American chances will rest with the college players who make the national team. Them and history.

Completing a double play against the U.S. at the 1990 Goodwill Games, second-baseman Antonio Pacheco is part of the exceptional talent that has brought Cuba 16 World Championships.

David Madison

BASKETBALL

By Larry Eldridge

- MEN'S EVENT
- WOMEN'S EVENT

The most dominating presence in professional basketball, Michael Jordan of the Chicago Bulls seems to spend much of his time on the court several feet above everybody else.

Rick Stewart / Allsport

The dream tournament basketball fans have longed for all these years becomes a reality this summer as American NBA stars battle the rest of the world's elite in the first-ever open Olympic competition.

Although injuries or last minute defections might change the roster before the Barcelona Games, the following NBA players were chosen for the U.S. team: Michael Jordan, Magic Johnson, Charles Barkley, Larry Bird, Scottie Pippen, John Stockton, Karl Malone, David Robinson, Patrick Ewing and Chris Mullin. Never before, it is safe to say, has such a talented squad been assembled for an Olympic basketball tournament.

Even if he doesn't play, Magic Johnson will be an inspiration for the U.S. team.

"The hypocrisy has finally ended," said Dave Gavitt, president of USA Basketball, the sport's governing body in the United States, in reference to the recent rule changes permitting such a scenario. "For the first time ever, we, like every other country, are allowed to draw from all our citizens. No longer is it America's best 19- to 21-year-olds against far more experienced veterans from other countries."

The former rules always did seem something out of *Alice in Wonderland*. If you played basketball for money in the NBA, you were a pro and therefore ineligible for the Olympics. But if you did the same thing anywhere else, it was okay.

Even with this handicap, of course, the Americans fared pretty well over the years. Their greater speed, mobility and overall skill were generally enough to overcome the advantages of experience, team cohesion and familiarity with international rules enjoyed by the national squads of other countries.

From the inaugural Olympic basketball competition at Berlin in 1936 through the Montreal Games 40 years later, U.S. domination was virtually total. The Americans won eight gold medals in nine

Larry Eldridge, former sports editor of The Christian Science Monitor, *has covered basketball for more than thirty years. He currently hosts his own national weekly TV show, "Eldridge on Sports."*

tries during that span, a record marred only by a still-controversial 51-50 loss to the Soviet Union in 1972, when the clock kept getting set back until the Soviets finally scored their decisive "buzzer beating" basket.

Indeed, throughout the 1950s and '60s, even without pros, the U.S. was virtually able to name the score in most of its games. But 1972 served notice that times were changing, for even if the outcome was questionable, the closeness of the score offered undeniable proof that the Americans were no longer invincible.

An interesting trivia question, in fact, is to name the only nation that has won men's basketball medals in the last four Olympics. The answer is neither the U.S. nor the U.S.S.R., but Yugoslavia.

Of course that's a trick question: The U.S. boycotted the '80 Games, and the Soviets returned the favor four years later at Los Angeles. Still, the Yugoslavs' record of one gold, two silvers and one bronze gives ample evidence of their strength and consistency — especially the gold, which was won in the Soviets' home court in 1980. And this year's team is expected to keep the string alive.

Until a civil war erupted last year, it appeared that Yugoslavia would be the United States' toughest opponent at the 1992 Games. The roster had several players with NBA credentials, including

Croatian Toni Kukoc led Yugoslavia to the 1991 European Championship, but may not compete on the Yugoslavian team at Barcelona.

Vlade Divac of the Los Angeles Lakers and Drazen Petrovic of the New Jersey Nets, plus, as Gavitt put it, "another player any NBA team would love to have" — Toni Kukoc, whom the champion Chicago Bulls have been trying unsuccessfully to lure away from Europe for quite some time. But the war has shattered the team's makeup. Ethnic conflict in Yugoslavia means that as of this writing, the national team will not include its two Croatian stars, Kukoc and Petrovic. With Divac at center, Yugoslavia will still be a medal contender, but no longer the power it was originally thought to be.

With 10 of the NBA's best players appearing on the U.S. team, the Americans have to rule as a strong favorite. Evaluating the other leading contenders gets more complicated. The U.S.S.R.'s tranformation into the Commonwealth of Independent States brings with it much uncertainty. While there almost surely will be a unified C.I.S. team, it is also possible that some of the Republics might try to field

Magic Johnson shocked not only Laker fans but the entire world with the announcement in November of his illness and his retirement from professional basketball.

55

Three-time Most Valuable Player in the NBA, Larry Bird has been doing it all for the Boston Celtics for 13 years.

their own squads. In addition, it is not clear how willing players from the separate Republics will be to participate on a Commonwealth team.

Prime examples are 6'11" longtime star center Arvydas Sabonis and Sarunas Marciulionis, who plays in the NBA for the Golden State Warriors and was the U.S.S.R.'s key player in its drive to the gold medal in Seoul. Both are Lithuanian, and even before Lithuania regained its independence both had declined to play for the Soviets in last year's European Championships. Without them the U.S.S.R. was never in contention.

Whatever the makeup of a new C.I.S. team, it is hard to imagine it being strong enough to advance to the finals — presumably to encounter the U.S.

The outside shooting of Golden State Warrior Chris Mullin should help the U.S. break the zone defenses it will confront in Barcelona.

But then, strange as it seems, there hasn't actually been such a game since that controversial Munich showdown in 1972. With the U.S. looking for revenge four years later in Montreal, the Yugoslavs took the opportunity away by getting a crack at the Soviets first and upsetting them in the semifinals. Then came the 1980 and 1984 boycotts, and when the U.S. finally met the U.S.S.R. in the 1988 Games, it was in the semifinals rather than the finals. The Soviet victory in Seoul meant that the last time the United States beat the U.S.S.R. in an Olympic basketball game of any sort was 1968.

Clearly, going by the results of these last several Olympics, it's been pretty much a question of the Big Three battling for the medals, with everyone else fighting for fourth place. But this time there are at least four other countries capable of pulling off an upset and maybe even sneaking into the medal picture.

Any team with a spectacular scorer like Brazil's Oscar Schmidt has to be reckoned with, since on his hottest nights he can practically win a game all by himself. Americans are still shaking their heads over his incredible 46-point performance that carried his team to victory over the U.S. in the 1987 Pan Am Games.

Australia has Andrew Gaze, well known to U.S. fans as one of the stars of that Cinderella Seton Hall team that went to the NCAA Final Four a couple of years ago.

Then there's Spain, which regularly fields a solid team anyway, and obviously will have the incentive of playing before a wildly partisan crowd cheering for the home team in its every game.

As for what will happen on the court when the games begin, tactics are expected to play an important role as usual. Coaches are always trying to come up with something new, and it will be interesting to see how some of them try this time to cope with the "talent gap."

> *The U.S. will almost certainly face zone defenses, prohibited in the NBA.*

"We'll see a lot of zones," says Gavitt — a pretty safe prediction, since the NBA players who make up the bulk of the U.S. team aren't used to this type of defense. This puts a premium on sharpshooters, of course, since outside shooting is the classic method of beating a zone, a factor that was obviously carefully considered by the committee selecting the U.S. team.

When U.S. opponents have the ball, Gavitt expects to see a barrage of 3-point shots regardless of what sort of defense the Americans use. He notes that the Europeans are particularly adept at 3-pointers, which in international play are taken from a line several feet closer than the NBA's, and only about nine inches farther out than the relatively easy U.S. college circle.

"Some of the teams we face will be shooting 3-pointers around 50 percent of the time," he said.

◆ **INTERNATIONAL RULES** ◆

While U.S. and international rules are essentially the same, there are some differences that U.S. players (and television viewers) must deal with:

Traveling: International rules allow a player an extra step if he is on the move when he receives the ball. This frequently confuses Americans, who think an opponent is taking too many steps, only to see him keep going and not get called for traveling. The U.S. coaches say it's difficult to ask players to change their offensive patterns to take advantage of this difference, and probably not that important; but it's critical, of course, for the American players to adjust defensively.

The 30-second clock: The team in possession must shoot for a basket within 30 seconds after gaining control, or the ball goes over to the other team. This is not the problem it once was, since the pros who will be playing for the U.S. this time are used to a 24-second clock, while the American collegians chosen for the team will just have to speed up their pace from the NCAA's 45-second version.

Timeouts: Each team gets only two per half, as compared to the five per game in college and seven in pro basketball, thus reducing the opportunity to use timeouts for tactical reasons.

Fouls: Each team is allowed seven fouls in each half before bonus free throws go into effect. In the NBA, penalty free throws begin after four team fouls (not including offensive fouls) are committed in each quarter.

Goaltending: Once the ball strikes the rim, either team can touch it, trying to knock it into or away from the basket — actions that would constitute illegal goaltending in many cases in the U.S.

No amount of strategic or technical adjustment, however, should prevent the brilliant U.S. players from winning the gold. The drama in men's basketball at Barcelona will be for the bronze and silver.

The experience Vlade Divac (right) has gained playing for the L.A. Lakers against NBA centers like David Robinson and Patrick Ewing will be an asset for Yugoslavia.

THE WOMEN'S COMPETITION

Teresa Edwards scored 18 points to lead the U.S. over Yugoslavia in the Seoul finals. The Americans are counting on her for another strong performance.

In women's basketball, the pendulum of power has swung dramatically from the Soviet Union to the United States over the past 10 years or so.

"Back in the '70s, everything we did was emulating the Soviets, trying to catch them," says Bill Wall, who as executive director of USA Basketball has been closely involved with the women's program for many years.

"But now it's they who are trying to emulate us, especially our quickness and the up-tempo game we play — things like full-court pressure, the fast break and the transition game."

Women's basketball was only added to the Olympics in 1976, and the U.S.S.R., then the world's strongest team by a huge margin, won that initial competition pretty much as it pleased. That's when the Americans began their chase, and by 1980 they felt the gap had been narrowed enough at least to make things interesting. We'll never know for sure, though, because the Moscow boycott interfered,

The smooth all-around play of Paola da Silva helped Brazil upset the U.S. at the 1991 Pan Am Games.

and with the U.S. out of the way the Soviets romped even more easily than they had in Montreal.

The results of other international competitions gave evidence, though, that "the Americans are coming." Beginning in 1979, the U.S. won three out of four World Championships. The Americans also won their first Olympic gold in 1984 (though with the Soviets absent), then repeated in 1988 at Seoul when everybody was there.

At Barcelona, the U.S. is certainly a strong candidate to make it three gold medals in a row, although their losses in the 1991 Pan Am Games to Brazil and Cuba make clear that they will not have an easy time of it. The former Soviets still pose a threat, but ever since the retirement of the great 7-foot center Yuliana Semyenova, they have just not been the same.

"There was a time when they just seemed to keep getting stronger and stronger," says Wall. At one point, in fact, the U.S.S.R. went 17 years without a loss in international competition. "It wasn't just Semyenova, it was the supporting cast, too. They played well together, and we frequently had to give away too much size at too many positions."

But as Wall puts it, "All of a sudden our talent level went up — and the Soviets got old."

◆ THE IMPROVED U.S. WOMEN ◆

There are several reasons for the American improvement: greater emphasis on the women's game in U.S. high schools and colleges; better coaching; more money for development programs; and more opportunities for international competition. And it's not just the United States that has gotten better; other countries have moved into the picture as well.

Indeed, it was Yugoslavia that finished second to the U.S. in the 1990 World Championships, with Cuba third — and both of these teams certainly must be reckoned with at Barcelona. Also hoping to be in the medal hunt are Australia and Brazil, the latter led by the fabulous Hortencia Marcari, considered by most observers the outstanding individual player in the women's game today, as well as Paola da Silva. Brazil's upset victory over the U.S. in an early round of the '91 Pan Am Games suggests how intense the competition at Barcelona will be.

The U.S. team will consist, as usual, of a group of experienced post-collegians, enhanced by a few of last season's top college performers. Talented players available include former Georgia teammates Teresa Edwards and Katrina McClain as well as Andrea Lloyd from Texas, all of whom played on the gold-medal 1988 team at Seoul. Lynette Woodard from Kansas, the first female member of the Harlem Globetrotters, will also be competing for a berth. Woodard made the 1980 team that had to miss Moscow, was co-captain in 1984, missed 1988 and would love to play in 1992.

Theresa Grentz of Rutgers University, who already has coached U.S. national teams to two gold medals (the World Championships and the Goodwill Games in 1990), will be directing the women's efforts to gain their third consecutive Olympic title.

Graceful Katrina McClain floats in for a lay-up against Cuba in the 1988 Games.

BOXING

By Michael Shapiro

MEN
Light Flyweight: 48kg/106lbs
Flyweight: 51kg/112lbs
Bantamweight: 54kg/119lbs
Featherweight: 57kg/125lbs
Lightweight: 60kg/132lbs
Light Welterweight: 63.5kg/139lbs
Welterweight: 67kg/147lbs
Light Middleweight: 71kg/156lbs
Middleweight: 75kg/165lbs
Light Heavyweight: 81kg/178lbs
Heavyweight: 91kg/201lbs
Super Heavyweight: +91kg/+201lbs

David Madison

Although Cuba's Orestes Solano (in red) lost to Germany's Sven Ottke at the World Cup Challenge in Bangkok, he is still a strong favorite for the light heavyweight gold at Barcelona.

Olympic boxing has produced glowing images which remain with us: the brash Cassius Clay winning a gold medal as a teenager in the 1960 Games before going on to become the legendary Muhammad Ali; George Foreman parading around the ring with a small American flag after his 1968 heavyweight victory; the elegant and graceful Sugar Ray Leonard leading five U.S. boxers to gold medals at the 1976 Olympics.

Along with the strong performances of the U.S. boxers, who captured eight medals, the Seoul Games were memorable for something else — controversy. A riot erupted when a group of South Korean boxing officials stormed the ring and attacked a referee from New Zealand after his warnings cost their fighter a bout. But the image that endures is that of South Korean Park Si-Hun with a gold medal draped around his neck, while below him, bearing silver, stood Roy Jones of the U.S.

That Jones won their fight and the gold was hardly in dispute. Still, the prize went to Park. The judges gave it to him. Amidst rumors of payoffs came this explanation from a Moroccan judge, who had scored the fight for Park. The judge, it seems, thought Jones's victory so overwhelming that he made the Korean the winner, thereby hoping to spare the local hero the ignominy of a loss by unanimous decision.

This explanation pleased no one, especially not Juan Antonio Samaranch, president of the IOC, who declared that unless amateur boxing cleaned up its act, it risked banishment from the Games.

The sport's elders, having heeded Samaranch's dictum, set to work — just as they did after the 1952 Games, when they faced the same sentence after an Olympic tournament marred by one-sided bouts, far too many knockouts and much too much blood. Forty years ago, the measures taken were designed to protect the boxers from each other, with the introduction of such rules as the standing eight-count and the end of extra points for knockdowns.

This time the measures are to protect the boxers from the judges. The result is that the sport the world watches in Barcelona will, in several

Michael Shapiro, author of books on Korea and Japan, has written about boxing for The New York Times *and* Sports Illustrated. *His work is included in Joyce Carol Oates' anthology on boxing,* Reading the Fights.

essential ways, differ from what was seen in Seoul.

To appreciate the changes, we must first understand how Olympic boxing differs from professional boxing, also known as prize fighting. Prize fights can last anywhere from four to 12 rounds. Amateur bouts last only three rounds. As in the professional game, each round lasts three minutes, with a minute's rest in between.

Elegant combinations will count less than clear, decisive punching.

The shorter bout means the amateur is tested in ways the pro is not. The amateur does not have the luxury of feeling out his opponent. He cannot afford to coast or lag for a round. He has to score points and score them in a space of only nine minutes. And then he has to be ready to fight again in a matter of days.

Points are earned when a boxer hits his opponent with a clean blow delivered by the fist area above and below the knuckles. To enable the judges to see whether the blow landed true, the amateur boxer's gloves are marked in white along the punching zone. Amateurs can be penalized for hitting below the belt, striking an opponent with an open hand, head butting or lying against the ropes.

Olympic boxers are divided by 12 weight categories, ranging from light flyweight — 48 kg — to super heavyweight — over 91 kg. Boxers in the six lighter divisions wear 10-ounce gloves; those in the heavier six divisions wear 12-ounce gloves. There is one other key difference between amateurs and professionals: The former wear protective headgear; the latter do not.

While professional boxing celebrates the knockdown — and knockout — amateur boxing generously rewards the jab. Knockouts can end an amateur fight, as can three knockdowns in a round, or four in a bout. But a fighter with a stiff jab can rack up many more points than a brawler looking to land one decisive blow.

And while that is scoring in its ideal form, the reality has been more problematic. Unlike swimming, where margins of victory are objectively determined, boxing has always been subjectively evaluated. Olympic boxing has been scored by five judges sitting at ringside, tallying blows, assessing

Light flyweight world champion Eric Griffin of the U.S. has lost only one bout since 1988 and doesn't plan on losing any more.

20 points to the winner of a round and up to 19 for the loser — and declaring who has won the bout.

The problem with judges, however, is that they are human and therefore imperfect. They might see the fight wrong, or they might *want* to see the fight wrong.

How, then, to make the judges accountable, or at least lessen the chances of poor judgment, error or chicanery? The answer, which has been around in Europe for more than 20 years, will be introduced to the Olympics in Barcelona: electronic scoring.

It works like this: Each judge has a console with scoring buttons for both boxers. When a boxer lands a scoring blow, the judge presses the appropriate button. If three of the five judges press their buttons within a second of each other — presumably within a second, too, of the blow landing — the fighter who threw the punch is awarded a point. At the end of the fight the man with the most points — having landed the most blows — wins. The system attempts to ensure that at the moment a clear blow lands, a fighter will receive credit and not be subject to the whim of a judge awarding points at the conclusion of a round. It is as close as boxing has yet come to being objective — the objectivity in this case belonging to the computer that keeps the score and, at the bout's conclusion, tallies up the points and declares a winner.

No one is suggesting that the system is perfect. A judge, for instance, could deliberately delay scoring a blow by half a second — count one thousand and one — but still show that he was not withholding points from the man in question: The computer just never counted them in its tally of scoring blows. A conscientious judge could also inadvertently be a half-beat slow in pressing his button, thereby possibly denying a boxer a point.

Still, "It's an honest attempt to rid the organization of some of its ills," says Jerry Dusenberry, vice president of the United States Amateur Boxing Federation.

It became Dusenberry's reponsibility to introduce the new scoring system to America's boxers, and to do so in a hurry: Fighters from Germany and the C.I.S., by contrast, have been familiar with electronic scoring, although primarily in minor dual meets, for years. The Americans are not enamored of the new system, in good measure because it works against what American fighters do best — dazzling combinations of punches swiftly delivered — and rewards the skills of their opponents.

Three-time gold-medalist Teofilo Stevenson embodies the glory of the Cuban boxing tradition.

A flashy boxer of the Sugar Ray Leonard variety, for instance, would have a rough time with the scoring machine. A fighter like Leonard lands many punches in a hurry, hitting his opponent far more quickly than the judges can hit their scoring buttons. The result is that an impressive flurry might go largely unrewarded. In contrast, the neat, cleanly executed right lead that his more plodding opponent might land would surely be noticed. And in-fighting — the blows boxers throw when

Oscar De La Hoya (right) has recently moved up from featherweight to become a prime U.S. medal hope at lightweight.

David Madison

they are nose to nose — might lack sufficient clarity to sway three judges.

◆ THE INDOMITABLE CUBANS ◆

"It does hurt our kids' speed because they're way ahead of the machines," says Pat Nappi, U.S. national boxing coach.

Still, it is for the machine that the Americans must prepare — the machine and the Cubans, who, even without the new rules, can make it difficult for anyone else to bring home the gold.

While the C.I.S. and Germany continue to produce top-rated boxers, and while the South Koreans showed themselves in Seoul to be a new force in the sport, amateur boxing remains a game dominated by Cuba. At the 1990 World Cup tournament held at three different sites, for instance, the Cubans won 10 out of 12 championships. The only American medalist was Eric Griffin, a light-flyweight from Houston who defeated Cuba's Orlando Asencio.

The lone American world champion in 1991 was Griffin, who along with lightweight Oscar De La Hoya of Los Angeles and bantamweight Sergio Reyes of the U.S. Marine Corps represent three of America's top boxing prospects in 1992.

The Americans will likely encounter such opponents as Cubans Felix Savon, a heavyweight, Juan Hernandez, a welterweight, and Orestes Solano (who, though the world's top-ranked amateur middleweight in 1990, still lost to Germany's Sven Ottke in Bangkok); Konstantin Tsiu, a light welterweight from the C.I.S.; Italian middleweight Tommaso Russo; Bulgarian featherweight Krikor Kikorov; and light heavyweight Torsten May from Germany.

But more than the fighters themselves, Nappi says, the Americans will be fighting their own perceptions of their opponents. The Americans are often younger than their Cuban or European opponents, and often far less experienced in international competition. The American team, after all, turns over every four years, with the best of the squad using their medals as springboards for professional careers.

The Cubans, on the other hand, tend to stay together. While the cushy existence of the well-subsidized Eastern European amateur is threatened by the new realities of democratization — and the curtailment of state funding for athletics — the Cubans remain cloistered and pampered.

And despite the fact that the most recent Cuban champions have stayed amateurs, still they constitute the stuff of legend — as in the case of three-time Olympic super heavyweight champion Teofilo Stevenson.

It is that tradition — and the myths of invincibility it generates — that Nappi must prepare his boxers to overcome.

"They are human," he says of the competition, adding that his boxers "will have to find that out for themselves."

Three-time world champion Felix Savon of Cuba intends to write his boxing memoirs after competing for the heavyweight gold in Barcelona.

DIVING

By Sharon Robb

MEN
Platform
Springboard

WOMEN
Platform
Springboard

Sun Shuwei of China, 1991 platform world champion, is a strong candidate to follow Greg Louganis as Olympic gold medalist.

American Kent Ferguson approaches the edge of the springboard. He stops and focuses his energy. Then in one explosive jump he takes off, creating a blur of twists and somersaults that somehow ends in a perfect vertical entry. A few bubbles come to the surface, the only vestige of a strong and graceful dive.

"It's a combination of athleticism and artistry and trying to maintain your confidence," says Ferguson, the world three-meter springboard champion and part-time fashion model. "You're up there on the board, trying to relax. All you're thinking about is enjoying the feeling — just let the dive flow and your mind and body will react."

Despite the simplicity of feeling Ferguson describes, diving is so extraordinarily complicated that an examination of every movement of even the plainest dive would read like a thesis on physiology and physics. Yet paradoxically, a dive happens so quickly it is often hard to focus clearly on its major features.

Judging the now-you-see-them-now-you-don't sport of diving doesn't take as much a critical eye as a discerning one. Although you can't expect to see things on television exactly as the judges at Barcelona will see them, it should help to have an idea of what they will be looking for. The seven judges generally will apply the following four criteria to each dive on the springboard and platform:

Height of the dive: The higher a diver goes, the better the dive is scored. Retired American gold-medalist Greg Louganis was considered the standard for this. "He got a foot higher than any other diver," according to six-time U.S. Olympic coach Ron O'Brien.

Mechanics: How well the diver carries through with the chosen dive and the distance from the water at which all maneuvers are completed. If one diver finishes a dive six feet above the water and another just before breaking the surface, for example, the first will earn a better score.

Positioning: Judges scrutinize the diver's form for such factors as pointed toes, arc of the back or straightened legs, depending on the chosen dive.

Sharon Robb, senior staff writer for The Fort Lauderdale News *and* The Sun-Sentinel, *has covered Olympic swimming and diving since 1981. She has written extensively for other publications, including* The Olympian *magazine.*

Distance from the board and the entry: Divers should hit the water three to five feet from the end of the board, following a smooth arc into the water. The body should be perfectly vertical as it breaks the surface.

Of all the different parts of the dive, the entry into the water is certainly the most important. Divers

> *"For the past few years, judges have been emphasizing ripping as an essential part of the entry," says Ron O'Brien.*

today have a tough time winning without producing a good "rip" at the end of the dive — the sound generated when divers break the water hands first and rip open as large a hole as possible, permitting the body to slip in cleanly with little splash. "Sounds like this," says O'Brien, tearing a sheet of paper in half.

Don't be misled by the elegance of a smooth entry into thinking that diving is a gentle, risk-free pastime. Hitting the water at approximately 33 miles per hour can produce injured fingers, arms and shoulders. When Ferguson slightly misjudged his distance at the 1988 Olympic trials and took the impact of the water on his shoulders rather than his hands, he ended up needing reconstructive surgery on his dislocated left shoulder. For Ferguson, "The injuries are part of the sport. The constant impact, particularly from platform, can take its toll on you. At times, you feel like you're falling off a building."

A new era in diving began the day after the 1988 Seoul Olympics, when Greg Louganis, arguably the best diver of all time, retired.

The absence of Louganis has created a void which the rest of the world, particularly the People's Republic of China, is rushing to fill. The Chinese are recognized as today's dominant diving power. They have become masters of executing precise and complex diving movements, their compact physiques giving them a spinning ability which enables them to enter the water cleanly without a ripple.

Xiong Ni and Sun Shuwei of China may well inherit Louganis's platform throne. Their lithe, muscular bodies, combined with their flexibility and intense concentration, give them the ability to

Irina Lashko of the C.I.S. poses a threat to Chinese dominance of the women's springboard.

Former wrestler Mark Lenzi of the U.S., the first diver ever to earn 100 points on a single dive, will have to be at his best to beat the Chinese for a springboard medal.

correct an error in mid-dive.

Xiong Ni, now 17, who was denied the gold at Seoul on an extraordinary final dive by Louganis, was platform gold medalist at the 1989 FINA World Cup in Indianapolis. Sun, 15, already has a World Championship and FINA World Cup gold medal tucked away.

Both will be challenged by Germany's Jan Hempel; Mexico's Fernando Platas and Jesus Mena; the C.I.S.'s Dmitry Sautin and Vladimir Timoshinin; and Canada's David Bédard. The U.S. men's platform hopes currently rest with national champion Scott Donie, Matt Scoggin, Pat Evans and Patrick Jeffrey, a member of the 1988 Olympic team, among others.

In the men's springboard, China's two-time silver medalist, Tan Liangde, will try to follow Louganis to the gold. Tan, at 27, is China's oldest springboard diver, leading his teammates Wang Yijie, 22, and Lan Wei, 23.

Along with world champion Ferguson, 22-year-old Mark Lenzi poses a legitimate threat to China's quest for the springboard gold. Wrestler-turned-diver Lenzi has already accomplished something that not even his idol, Louganis, ever managed: Lenzi became the first person in the history of the sport to earn 100 points on a single springboard dive, scoring 101.85 on a reverse three-and-one-half somersault from the tuck position.

Lenzi and Ferguson will be pushed by several veteran U.S. divers, including Pat Evans and '88 Olympian Mark Bradshaw. Germany's World Cup silver medalist, Albin Killat, and Hempel have hopes of taking home their country's Olympic medals.

With defending Olympic gold medalists Xu Yanmei and Gao Min returning, the Chinese are at the top in the women's platform and springboard events as well. Their strength includes 1991 world platform champion Fu Mingxia, who at 4' and 77 pounds became the youngest gold medalist ever at the World Championships, setting a record which will probably never be broken. Only 12 when she dazzled the judges with her talent, her youth also sent the FINA technical diving committee into a tailspin. Concerned with the safety of young bodies, the committee ruled that to compete divers must be 14 during the calendar year of Olympic, World Championship or World Cup competition.

The biggest challenge to China comes from the Commonwealth's Irina Lashko on springboard and Elena Miroshima on platform. The C.I.S. has borrowed the Chinese tactic of handpicking young gymnasts from the gymnasium floor and putting them into the diving well.

Still, don't count the U.S. out with '88 Olympic bronze-medalist Wendy Williams, the female version of Louganis with her model-good looks, grace and fluidity. Williams is heads above the U.S. platform field that includes current and former national

Mark Lenzi is currently the only diver in the world to have a 4½ somersault tuck on his springboard list.

champions Cokey Smith and Mary Ellen Clark.

1988 U.S. Olympian Wendy Lucero-Schayes, Germany's Doerte Lindner and Brita Baldus, gold medalist at the '91 World Cup, as well as Czechoslovakia's Heidemarie Bartova add to the excitement on springboard.

A total of 87 different dives are approved for competition. The springboard groups include forward, back, reverse, inward and twist. The platform dives are the same, with the addition of the

Kent Ferguson, part-time fashion model, is a full-time U.S. springboard diver, holder of five national and 15 international titles.

Gao Min of China hopes to win her second consecutive Olympic gold medal in springboard at Barcelona.

armstand group in which the divers start from a handstand position.

Once in the air, the diver's body is straight, pike or tuck. In the straight position, arms must be fully extended and feet together. In the pike, the body is bent at the waist, but knees are straight. In the tuck, both waist and knees are bent, with knees together. The toes are pointed in all three. The free position, used in twisting dives, is a combination of two of the others.

Women perform 10 dives on springboard (five required, five optional) and eight on platform (four required, four optional). Men complete 11 dives on springboard (five required, six optional) and 10 on platform (four required, six optional). Divers are required to give written notice of the dives they will attempt at least 24 hours in advance of the competition.

For purposes of scoring, dives are assigned different degrees of difficulty. The higher the D.D., the higher the potential score, but also greater the danger of failure. Many divers choose to play it safe, nailing lower D.D. dives rather than risking a bungled high D.D. This explains why Lenzi will not include his reverse three-and-one-half somersault tuck until he is absolutely confident he can manage it. "If it's there, I'll use it, but I won't blow my whole list for a dive I can't nail," Lenzi said.

The process of scoring occurs as follows: After each dive the seven judges award points ranging from 10 to 0. The highest and lowest scores are then eliminated to minimize possible judging biases. The five remaining scores are totaled and multiplied by the degree of difficulty. The result is then multiplied by .6 to produce the rating for the particular dive.

Even though there are certain criteria of execution which all divers must meet, evaluation still remains a highly subjective process. No matter how well a dive is performed, the individual artistic sensibilities of those judging will necessarily play a large part in determining the score. Inevitably there will be differences of opinion among coaches, competitors, judges and spectators regarding the excellence of any given dive.

However subjective the judgments, you can be sure of one objective fact: Olympic diving will present an extraordinary spectacle of courage, grace, strength and agility as superb athletes plunge into the water in pursuit of the gold.

EQUESTRIAN

By Nancy Jaffer

Individual Dressage
Individual Show Jumping
Individual Three-day Event
Team Dressage
Team Show Jumping
Team Three-day Event

Greg Best, winner of a silver medal on Gem Twist in both the individual and team jumping at the 1988 Games, is the U.S. team's premier show jumper.

Nancie Battaglia

Equestrian sports extend the conventional understanding of teamwork beyond the strictly human realm to the delicate relationship of horse and rider. Cooperation between the two is a product of intense preparation, the reward of a daily routine often pursued for years before human and animal can function as one unit. No one can simply acquire a great mount and expect it to perform. Relationships can only be built on experience and compromise.

Equestrian is one of three Olympic sports (shooting and yachting are the others) in which men and women compete as equals. As tact is often more important than pure strength, women claim a fair share of medals in each of the three Olympic equestrian disciplines: show jumping, dressage and three-day eventing.

Show jumping, the best known of the three, is easy to understand. Competitors must clear 17 or so colorful obstacles up to approximately 5'3" high and 6'6" wide within a designated time. Penalty points are incurred if a horse dislodges an obstacle rail in the process of jumping over it, or refuses to attempt a jump at a particular obstacle. The rider with the fewest penalty points wins.

In the case of jumpers finishing with an identical number of penalty points, the medal goes to the rider who has completed the course in the fastest time.

The speed and daring of show jumping have their artistic counterpoint in dressage, in which elegance and control are critical for success. Five judges award points on a scale of 1 to 10 as they evaluate the precision with which riders take their mounts through a number of different movements. In addition to a basic walk, trot and canter, horses must perform the *passage* (a slow, stylized trot); the *piaffe* (in which they prance in place); and pirouettes.

Judges look at both the skill of the horse and its flair in completing each exercise as it responds obediently to the rider's non-verbal commands.

Three-day eventing combines dressage (the first day) and show jumping (the last day). Both are scaled-down versions of the Olympic events that stand alone.

Nancy Jaffer, equestrian columnist for the Newark Star-Ledger, *has covered the equestrian events in the last two Olympics and all World Championships since 1982.*

Between the two is the heart of eventing, its speed and endurance phase, consisting of three different trials: the first, a course of 16 to 20 kilometers of roads and tracks; second, a steeplechase ranging from 3.1 to 3.4 km; and last, a cross-country route of 7.4 to 7.7 km. All must be completed within specified times or penalty points are assessed. The rider with the fewest penalty points wins. Performance in this phase of eventing is weighted more heavily than the other two days' achievements in compiling the final scores.

Bravery, endurance and athletic ability are tested during the cross-country run, which requires horse and rider to clear approximately 32 solid barriers up to 3'9" high. Littered with water obstacles, ditches and multi-part obstacles, the course offers difficulties limited only by the designer's imagination.

Europe and the United States have traditionally dominated the medal ranks in equestrian events, and 1992 should be no different.

The speed and daring of show jumping have their artistic counterpoint in dressage.

Show jumping enthusiasts expect to see American Greg Best, who rides the grey thoroughbred, Gem Twist, receive a medal when the individual show jumping awards are handed out in Barcelona. They should be challenged by two-time World Cup champion John Whitaker of Great Britain and another great grey, Henderson Milton, as well as France's world and European champion Eric Navet with the stallion Quito de Baussy.

The world champion French, the European champion Dutch, the Olympic champion Germans, the British and Americans should account for the team medals.

Dressage is the realm of the Europeans, most notably the Germans, who have taken the team and individual gold medals in the last two Olympics. If they fail to win this time, it will probably be as a result of a superior performance by the C.I.S., Switzerland or Sweden.

A strong possibility to repeat her individual gold medal is Germany's Nicole Uphoff, the youngest person ever to take such a title when she accomplished the feat at 21 in 1988 on Rembrandt. That combination also won the individual gold at the most recent World Championships in 1990.

In eventing, the battle for gold likely will involve Britain, a perennial powerhouse, and New Zealand, which took the team gold at the World Championships. Germany should be in the hunt and France is rising fast. An improving U.S. team might just be a threat in Barcelona.

On the individual side, New Zealand's world champion, Blythe Tate (Messiah), her teammate Mark Todd and Britain's Ian Stark (Murphy Himself) could be neck-and-neck for the gold. They were 1-2 in the World Championships, where America's two-time world champion Bruce Davidson was third on Pirate Lion. He is probably the best U.S. hope for individual honors.

If Germany's Nicole Uphoff wins the individual title in dressage, it won't be the surprise it was at Seoul when she became the youngest gold medalist ever in the sport.

GYMNASTICS

By Kent Hannon

MEN
Floor Exercise
High Bar
Pommel Horse
Vault
Parallel Bars
Rings
All-around
Team Competition

WOMEN
Floor Exercise
Uneven Bars
Balance Beam
Vault
All-around
Team Competition

Italy's Yuri Chechi is one of the few who could prevent another Soviet sweep of medals in the men's all-around.

Yann Guichaqua / Allsport

The Great Soviet Gymnastics Machine rolled into Seoul four years ago and made a shambles of the Olympic competition, winning 11 of the 18 gold medals awarded in the men's and women's divisions. The Soviets also carted away five silver medals and three bronze, giving them a total of 19 medals — more than their closest competitors, Romania (9) and East Germany (8), combined. "We did not want just a victory," said Soviet national coach Leonid Arkaev of his team's performance at the '88 Games. "We wanted to show we were on the peak of progress; we were dictating fashion."

When Arkaev speaks of the "peak of progress" and "dictating fashion," he refers to the highest level of difficulty that gymnasts can build into their routines to impress the judges and outdistance the opposition. This level of difficulty is always escalating — innovative maneuvers in one Olympics become everyday occurences by the next — and the '92 Games in Barcelona will doubtless be remembered for several daring new somersaults and high-bar releases.

The ever-evolving repertoire of moves is what makes gymnastics a genuine art form and separates it from a sport such as track and field. In the 100-meter dash, for example, a Carl Lewis can't simply *decide* to extend the limits of the sport with a sub-9.8; it has to *happen*, and even then the evaporation of time is not something most spectators can see or appreciate without checking the official clock. Whereas, if a high-bar worker wants to dismount with something totally new — a quadruple somersault, let's imagine — he can simply decide to do it. That doesn't necessarily mean he'll land it, but the chance that he might — or crash spectacularly trying — provides part of the appeal of gymnastics.

The overwhelming Soviet mastery of the '88 Olympics did not surprise anybody with a sense of gymnastics history. Soviet women have won every Olympic competition they have entered since the end of World War II, and the men have dominated the sport since the 1979 World Championships.

Despite the retirement of some of the former Soviet Union's brightest stars, Barcelona looks to be no different. Even without the likes of the women's all-around gold medalist at Seoul, Yelena Shushunova, and the brilliant Dmitry Bilozerchev, the C.I.S. still has superb athletes like Grigory Misutin, Vitaly Scherbo and Svetlana Boginskaya. Whoever represents it at Barcelona, the Commonwealth will be favored to win the team golds over China on the men's side and Romania on the women's. No other country can match the capacity of the former Soviets to include tremendous difficulty in their programs while maintaining quality and consistency — the key to their success, according to Bela Karolyi, former Romanian Olympic coach who now coaches in the United States.

The Romanian women remain strong, though they also have been hard hit by retirement. They will have to get along without Daniela Silivas (winner of six Olympic medals, three of them gold) and '87 world champion Aurelia Dobre. If the past is any indication, however, they will manage nicely, particularly with young talents like Cristina Bontas on the team.

Historically, the East Germans have nearly always been a factor in both men's and women's competition, but now that the wall is down, the newly united German team is an unknown quantity — but the men figure to be very good.

Kent Hannon, former staff writer for Sports Illustrated *who co-authored an award-winning book on gymnastics with Kurt Thomas, teaches journalism at the University of Georgia.*

Kim Zmeskal and Betty Okino

Kim Zmeskal and Betty Okino are alike in that both train at Bela Karolyi's gym in Houston; both have won the American Cup; both like to go to the movies; and each thinks the other is the favorite to win the gold medal in the all-around at Barcelona.

They're also different in many ways. Zmeskal is a little strawberry-blond who lives just a few blocks from Karolyi's gym, where she's trained since she was 6. Okino, on the other hand, elegant and dark-haired, hails from Elmhurst, Ill., and has only been with Karolyi for two years, rising from No. 20 in the U.S. to No. 2, behind Zmeskal. While Zmeskal's parents are American, Okino's father is Ugandan, and her mother, like Karolyi, is Romanian.

One final similarity that Karolyi notices: "You should see how they look at each other in practice," he says. "It doesn't matter who's up on the apparatus, Kim or Betty. You can tell from their eyes what the other is thinking: Did you see how well she did that move!"

The American men won't be in the hunt for medals in either team or individual competition. They haven't had a legitimate international star capable of beating top-flight gymnasts from the C.I.S., Germany or China since Kurt Thomas retired, following his unprecedented six-medal flourish at the '79 World Championships in Fort Worth, Texas.

But the fast-improving American women might just eke out a team medal and a few individual ones as well. They finished fourth at the 1988 Olympics and would have won the bronze medal if they hadn't been cited for an obscure rules violation.

Much of the American women's success can be attributed to Karolyi, who defected to the U.S. from Romania in 1981 and started his own gymnastics school in Houston. Karolyi's operation numbers

Vitaly Scherbo

With his freckled face, his boyish grin and his total lack of pretension, Vitaly Scherbo has more in common with, say, Huckleberry Finn than with the parade of exacting but unemotional Soviet gymnastics stars who have gone before him.

For example, when Scherbo saw his 9.9 score flashed at the conclusion of the high-bar competition at the '90 Goodwill Games, meaning he had tied for the gold medal, he pumped his fist in the air with joy.

"I couldn't hold back my emotions," says the 19-year-old Ukrainian, "although, generally speaking, I think it is unbecoming to act like you think you're a national hero."

Scherbo burst onto the international scene with three gold medals (floor, vault, high bar) at the '90 European Championships and won more medals (five) at the '91 Worlds in Indianapolis than anyone on the Soviet team.

Scherbo comes by his gymnastics talent naturally; both of his parents were acrobats. And when he isn't pumping his fists in the air, he's using them to break boards in his favorite pastime, kung fu.

---

roughly 700 girls, and as many as five of his elite pupils could make the six-member U.S. Olympic team. Heading Karolyi's current class of Barcelona hopefuls is 16-year-old Kim Zmeskal and 17-year-old Betty Okino, who, in Karolyi's mind, are co-favorites to win the gold medal in the all-around. Zmeskal's stunning victory in the 1991 World Championships — the first American, man or woman, ever to win the all-around title at the Worlds — represents an enormous achievement for the American gymnastics program.

Like Mary Lou Retton, Karolyi's first U.S. star, who won the all-around title at the Soviet-boycotted 1984 Games, Zmeskal, only 4'7" and 80 pounds, is a high-powered, bam-bam tumbler. When she won her first big international meet, the 1990 American Cup, the press dubbed her "Karolyi's latest bundle of energy." Zmeskal displays that energy best in floor-ex, which women always infuse with a healthy dose of dance. Zmeskal excels in that department, and her tumbling passes are as macho as any of the men's — who never, ever dance.

No matter whom you focus your attention on in the '92 Olympic competition, keep your eyes on the floor-ex mat and on the high bar and uneven bars because that's where the most sensational acrobatics will take place. A pair of equipment changes will accentuate those acrobatics.

"The most noticeable difference between the Seoul Olympics and Barcelona," says Karolyi, "is that the floor-ex mat has been made much springier to allow gymnasts to get greater height on their tumbling passes. The uneven bars have also been moved farther apart to allow women room to do giant swings, big release moves and exciting dismounts — just like the men do on high bar."

The fundamental gymnastics movement — the somersault — is the source of excitement in floor-ex, and both men and women perform these airborne "somies" or "saltos" in three different body positions: tuck (knees bent up against the chest), pike (body folded over like a jackknife in diving), layout (straight body and legs fully extended). Tuck is the easiest, layout the most difficult, and Zmeskal will show the judges at least one double back layout during her floor-ex routine. The Chinese are currently the most daring floor-ex practicioners, and if Li Chunyang is healthy in Barcelona, he might just try a triple back somersault.

One of the foremost high-bar workers in the world right now is Japan's Daisuke Nishikawa, who won a gold medal in that event at the '90 World Cup. Nishikawa is known for his novel dismount: a double back somersault with a double twist. On the uneven bars, Hungary's Henrietta Onodi incorporates two release moves in a routine which figures to include at least one "blind change" as she flies from the low bar to the high bar without looking.

As coach of the Romanian women, Bela Karolyi produced six Olympic and fourteen world champions.

Though they bear no resemblance to each other in terms of design and prerequisite body mechanics, balance beam and men's pommel horse are related in the sense that they are the most difficult apparatuses to master — mainly because it's so easy to fall off the four-inch-wide beam and the oddly shaped horse. It's here that both individual and team titles are often won and lost. But that doesn't mean you'll see a lot of caution exhibited, because caution is invariably what makes a gymnast fall.

Betty Okino, who finished fourth in the all-around at the '91 Worlds, has originated a balance beam move that unofficially bears her name; an "Okino" is a triple pirouette. To get an idea of how it feels to do an Okino on a four-inch-wide beam, climb up on the edge of your coffee table and try to spin around three times without landing in the hospital. The very nature of the pommel horse event — asking a man to support all his weight on his hands while he swings his legs in lateral circles, thus interfering with his hands' support position every half-second — seems to ask the impossible. But as difficult as the pommel horse is, watch the grace and speed with which 1991 world champion Valery Belenky of the C.I.S. travels up and down the horse, working on and off the pommels like a man trying to put a fire out with his hands.

The vault may appear to be the same event for both sexes, but the women turn it sideways and vault over its midsection, whereas the men must clear it lengthwise.

Pommel horse world champion Valery Belenky of the C.I.S. did not take up gymnastics until the relatively late age of 7, when his father became his first coach.

Bo Yang is part of the talent that makes the Chinese team the most innovative in floor-exercise competition.

of China spices up his p-bar routine with a 1¾ front somersault which he finishes by landing with arms astride the bars — and then carries on with the remainder of his routine.

◆ SCORING ◆

A 10.0 is the highest score gymnasts can receive, but explaining what they have to do to earn that 10.0 — other than to do everything perfectly — would require a long-winded summary of the Code of Points. Explaining how gymnasts lose points with the judges is much easier. For example, the idea is to "stick" each landing or dismount, meaning gymnasts want to stand stock-still when they unwind from a somersault, as opposed to hopping — because each hop means .1 off. Little breaks in form, such as bent arms or droopy legs mean .1 off. Touching hands to the floor to regain balance on a landing or dismount means .3 off. Using hands to prevent what otherwise would be a fall means .5 off. Falling off the apparatus means .5 off.

◆ TEAM COMPETITION ◆

Six gymnasts compete for each country, but a team's lowest score on each event is thrown out — thus, only five are counted. Women compete in four events (vault, uneven bars, balance beam, floor exercise), so their optimum team score is 50.0 points per event, or 200.0 for all four. Men compete in six events (floor exercise, pommel horse, rings, vault, parallel bars, high bar) with an optimum team score of 50.0 per event (300.0 for all six).

Team competition involves two rounds — compulsories (basic maneuvers) and optionals (sky's the limit!). The optimum team score is 400.0 points for the women and 600.0 for the men.

The men's and women's individual all-around features the top 36 scorers from the team competition, with no more than three from any one country. These 36 go through one four- or six-event round, the winners being declared the best all-around gymnasts in the world.

Individual event winners are determined by a separate competition which occurs after the team and all-around medals are decided.

The process of judging the performances is far from scientific. No two judges interpret the Code of Points the same way. It is a highly subjective enterprise fraught with the same differences of opinion that can crop up when a sliding base runner

Svetlana Boginskaya

Her teammates call her "The Goddess" because her movements are so elegant and her demeanor so regal. But to see her face — beautiful, yet frozen in sadness — is to know that Svetlana Boginskaya of Belarus has been touched by tragedy. Just three days after she won two gold medals at the 1988 Olympics, her coach was found dead; some reports indicated suicide.

"After my coach's death, I couldn't even make myself go into the gym," says Boginskaya, 19, who was born in Minsk.

A year later, on the eve of the '89 Worlds, Boginskaya had a falling out with her new coach. Managing nevertheless to win the all-around title, she then burst into tears on the victory stand.

"I suddenly felt lonely," she says. "I thought, 'Do I need this victory if there is no one with me to share my joy?' "

Her heartache continues: Upset over her loss to Kim Zmeskal in the all-around at the '91 Worlds in Indianapolis, Boginskaya refused to shake Zmeskal's hand at the awards ceremony. Would things have been different had the meet been held in Europe? Boginskaya replied, "I'm 100 percent sure of it."

Both the rings and the parallel bars used to be primarily muscle events with a lot of posing and static moments. And while rings are still known for those dramatic crosses — e.g., Maltese, Iron, Olympic — both of these men's events now incorporate more swinging moves. The former Soviets are the best ring-men in the world, so expect all sorts of wild, twisting dismounts from them. Li Jing

Hungary's Henrietta Onodi's vaulting flair brought her the silver at the 1991 World Championships.

If there's one constant that remains fixed in a gymnast's mind besides the unpredictability of judging, it's the risk of injury. Most gymnasts say publicly that they don't think about getting hurt, but Zmeskal and Okino both concede that the danger of crashing and burning on a trick is difficult to dismiss. The real achievement, they say, is to learn to practice and perform with pain.

"You know what they say — 'no pain, no gain' — well it's true," says Zmeskal, who has waged a long-term battle with a stress fracture in her wrist, which she says "will probably never be completely healed as long as I continue competing."

Zmeskal's sentiments explain why Karolyi doesn't flinch when asked about charges from some of his former pupils, who say he expected them to practice and compete while injured.

"There is a certain amount of truth to that," he says with an ironic smile, "because gymnastics is a sport where to succeed you have to take it as far as you can. There's often a fine line between an injury that's painful and one that should keep you out of a competition. I've never forced a gymnast to compete, but you have to go hard in this sport; it is no tea party."

and a throw to the catcher arrive at home plate at the same time. Except that the umpire's decision in baseball isn't colored by the kind of off-mat intrigues — i.e., East-West or gymnastics federation politics — which sometimes affect a gymnastics judge's decisions. The Americans have long complained about Eastern bloc judges "delivering" scores for athletes from Iron Curtain countries, while undervaluing U.S. competitors. Eastern bloc judges deny those charges, but the feud simmered anew at the '88 Games, when an East German judge penalized the American women for a technical violation regarding where team members are permitted to stand. As a result, the Americans lost the bronze medal — to the East Germans. Political changes in Eastern Europe might well minimize U.S. concerns in the future.

High-bar world champion Li Chunyang of China might surprise in the floor exercise should he successfully manage a difficult triple back somersault.

RHYTHMIC GYMNASTICS

By Dwight Normile

WOMEN'S EVENT

While rhythmic gymnastics only entered the Olympics in 1984, its roots can be traced back to the ancient Greeks, who developed it originally as an amusement for young girls. As a competitive sport for highly trained, dedicated athletes, rhythmic has been popular in Eastern Europe since the 1930s. It was officially recognized in 1962 by the International Gymnastics Federation.

The goal of the rhythmic gymnast is to create pure, harmonious movement, without acrobatics, to musical accompaniment. At Barcelona, the gymnasts will perform their four musical routines, each lasting between 60-90 seconds, with four different kinds of apparatus: rope, hoop, ball and clubs. (Every other year, one apparatus — in this case the ribbon — is rotated out of the competition.)

Working on a 40x40-foot (12x12-meter), carpeted floor space, performers must keep the apparatus moving at all times, except for accents, as they engage in their elegant, technically demanding routines. Skills must be executed with both hands. Gymnasts are required to perform movements while in the air (leaping), standing upright (dancing) and on the floor (rolling). With each separate apparatus, the competitor must include at least four elements of medium difficulty and four of superior difficulty.

The goal is to create pure, harmonious movement, without acrobatics, to musical accompaniment.

Part of the viewer's difficulty will be understanding the sometimes complicated distinction between the two. A simple instance will give the idea: Tossing the ball into the air and performing a double pirouette before catching it constitutes an element of superior difficulty. A toss with a single pirouette would be an example of medium difficulty.

In addition to the basic actions of throwing and catching, the characteristic movements with each apparatus you will see performed are as follows:

Dwight Normile, editor since 1982 of International Gymnast, *is a former national gymnastics competitor and judge.*

Rope: jumping with the rope open or folded, swinging and circling.

Hoop: turns, spins, rotations on the floor and around the hand or other parts of the body.

Ball: bouncing or rolling over different parts of the body.

Clubs: large and small circles, rhythmic tapping, swings.

Scoring is determined by two separate panels of four judges. One panel evaluates the composition of each competitor's routine, the other its technical execution. The maximum score for each routine is 10.0 (6.8 for composition, 3.2 for execution); performers are penalized if they drop the apparatus and lose additional points if they must leave the floor space to retrieve it.

◆ COMMUNICATING EMOTION ◆

Rhythmic gymnastics demands a variety of athletic talents, foremost among them the strength and agility of the ballet dancer. With the growing importance of high tosses and behind-the-back catches, the hand-eye coordination of the skilled juggler is also essential. But perhaps the most critical — if intangible — quality which the top gymnasts must possess is the capacity to express emotion through their movements. Each routine must convey a coherent emotional mood and evoke a response from the audience. A routine that leaves the audience indifferent will do the same to the judges.

The best in the world at convincing audience and judges alike are the Bulgarian and Commonwealth women. The Bulgarians dominated the sport throughout the '80s, but at Seoul the gold and bronze were won by Marina Lobatch and Aleksandra Timoshenko, respectively, of the C.I.S.

Lobatch and Seoul silver-medalist, Bulgarian Adriana Dounavska have retired from the sport, while Timoshenko has matured into a formidable competitor who has gathered a variety of titles since Seoul. Oksana Skaldina of the C.I.S., who won the 1990 World Cup, will certainly challenge Timoshenko for the gold at Barcelona, as will Bulgarian Julia Baicheva. Although Spain has been rapidly improving and will have the home-country advantage for inspiration, it is hard to imagine that the three medals will not once again be claimed by the Bulgarians and former Soviets.

From a traditionally strong Bulgarian team, Julia Baicheva continues to make a routine out of the impossible.

Second to her teammate Oksana Skaldina at the World Championships, Aleksandra Timoshenko of the C.I.S. will try to reverse that finish at the Games.

SOCCER

By Paul Gardner

MEN'S EVENT

Logically enough, soccer, the World's Most Popular Sport, tops the attendance charts at the Olympic Games, outdrawing all other sports by a wide margin.

Over 1.8 million fans turned out for the 32 soccer matches in the Soviet Union in 1980 — more than one-third of the total attendance for the entire Olympics. Even at the 1984 Los Angeles Games, in the supposedly soccer-resistant USA, soccer was No.1, pulling 1.4 million, to track's 1.1 million.

The big crowds — and the money that comes with them — have firmly established soccer as a key Olympic event. Yet, from a soccer point of view, the tournament is a bit of an ugly duckling — an ill-defined affair, doomed to an apologetic existence in the shadows of the vastly more important World Cup.

It was soccer's governing body, FIFA *(Federation Internationale de Football Association)*, that created the World Cup in 1930, realizing that the amateur Olympic tournament (which it also runs) could never be a representative competition in the increasingly professional world of international soccer.

At a stroke, Olympic soccer was cursed with a minor-league image. It was dropped in 1932, but returned in 1936 to be used as a political tool by the fascist dictatorships. Mussolini's Italy took the title, while Hitler suffered the embarrassment of watching Germany eliminated by lowly Norway. He never attended another soccer game.

After World War II, fascist influence was replaced by communist domination. Insisting that all of their players were amateurs, the Iron Curtain countries regularly fielded their full national teams in the Olympics.

The thing bordered on a farce. The major soccer powers, such as Brazil, Italy, West Germany and the Netherlands, were barred from using their stars, all of whom were professional. Hence, no Pele, no Gigi Riva, no Franz Beckenbauer, no Johan Cruyff, pros all of them. Inevitably, interest among the non-communist countries became lukewarm. They entered, at best, B-teams, and no one was surprised when they lost. Nobody beat the East Europeans — except other East Europeans.

◆ **EAST EUROPEAN DOMINATION** ◆

The upshot was a 28-year uninterrupted run of East European gold medals from 1952 until 1980. The Olympic soccer tournament had become the Championship of Communist Europe.

Trying to remain reasonably competitive, some of the non-communist countries cheated in a low-key sort of way by fielding young pros. After France (which was trying to field amateurs) had soundly beaten Mexico 4-1 in the 1968 Olympics, the French coach remarked to the press that it was always nice to beat the host team "and its professionals." The Mexican journalists protested — this was the Olympics, only amateurs were allowed. The coach scornfully silenced them with "Come, my friends, everyone knows …."

Everyone knew, but no action was taken until 1980 when FIFA struck at East European dominance by ruling out players who had participated in World Cup games. The inevitable arrived in 1984,

Claudio Reyna of the University of Virginia provides the offensive spark for a fast-improving U.S. team.

Paul Gardner, internationally acclaimed soccer writer and columnist for Soccer America, *is the author of* The Simplest Game.

when pros were — officially — admitted, though the ban on World Cup players remained.

Now the International Olympic Committee wanted to go whole hog, to do away with all restrictions, to have the Olympic tournament be, in effect, another World Cup.

FIFA was not having that and proposed instead an age limit of 23 years. When the IOC rejected that, FIFA threatened to take soccer out of the Olympics. The IOC — no doubt with an eye on those massive crowd figures — backed down, and FIFA got its way. The 16 finalists in Barcelona, qualifying on the basis of regional competitions throughout the world, will feature pros and amateurs alike — with only one restriction: All must be born on or after August 1, 1969.

As the World Under-23 Championship, Olympic soccer has, at long last, an identity. But it remains to be seen if the top European and South American pro clubs will take the tournament seriously enough to release their best young players.

If they do, then Olympic soccer will be freed from the East European stranglehold and the suffocating conformity of a rather mechanical vision of the game. The full, colorful mosaic of differing national styles will be on show, each now with a realistic chance of success.

The artistry and individual ball skills of the South Americans; the more straightforward but tactically disciplined Germans, always at their best in concentrated tournament play; the Italians, masters of defensive play allied to the sudden, deadly counter-attack; the emerging African nations, tactically a trifle naive, perhaps, but bristling with explosively exciting players. Even the East Europeans — as the Soviets showed in taking the 1988 gold medal — have a more enterprising, a more *glastnosty* look about their play these days. And the U.S., gaining confidence at the international level, but still a team in search of a style.

Predictions? In Olympic soccer? Well, just one — it will top the attendance charts again.

Brazil (in blue) defeated Germany 2-1 on its way to a silver medal at the 1988 Games.

SWIMMING

By John Powers

MEN
50m Freestyle
100m Freestyle
200m Freestyle
400m Freestyle
1,500m Freestyle
100m Breaststroke
200m Breaststroke
100m Butterfly
200m Butterfly
100m Backstroke
200m Backstroke
200m Medley
400m Medley
4x100m Freestyle Relay
4x200m Freestyle Relay
4x100m Medley Relay

WOMEN
50m Freestyle
100m Freestyle
200m Freestyle
400m Freestyle
800m Freestyle
100m Breaststroke
200m Breaststroke
100m Butterfly
200m Butterfly
100m Backstroke
200m Backstroke
200m Medley
400m Medley
4x100m Freestyle Relay
4x100m Medley Relay

No Olympic sport deals in instant obsolescence as much as swimming does. This year's colossus is next year's dust. Today's world champion can't make tomorrow's Olympic team. The morning's record-setter is beaten in the evening.

Four years ago, East Germany's women ruled the planet. Then the Berlin Wall came down and the German Democratic Republic vanished. In 1991, the East Germans, shorn of their subsidies on a combined Deutschland team, failed to win a single gold medal at the quadrennial World Championships in Perth, Australia.

Just that quickly does swimming's world order change. The American women, once resigned to slogging in East German backwash, suddenly find themselves back on top, chased by a hungry new pursuer — the Chinese. And the U.S. men, who won 27 medals in one Olympics as recently as 1976, will have to share the Barcelona stage with a quartet of challengers — from Germany, Hungary, the Commonwealth and Italy.

While some of the Seoul stars — Matt Biondi, Janet Evans, Tamas Darnyi, Krisztina Egerszegi and Anthony Nesty — will be on hand at this year's Summer Games, most have either retired or been eclipsed by newer, faster bodies.

"Swimming is a lot like nature," says Eddie Reese, who will coach the American men at Barcelona. "When there's a weakness or an opening, somebody fills it."

◆ THE CHANGING FAVORITES ◆

Of the 26 individual gold medalists in 1988, only five repeated in the 1991 World Championships, winning a total of seven events. Most of the new titleholders, now regarded as the current favorites, were unknown four years ago.

China's Li Lin, who won both individual medleys at Perth, didn't come close to medaling at Seoul. Hungary's Norbert Rozsa, who won the 100-meter breaststroke, was competing in his first major international meet. His female counterpart, Australia's Linley Frame, was ranked only 54th in the world. Nicole Haislett, who ended 18 years of East German dominance in the 100-meter freestyle, was one of

John Powers, 1982 Pulitzer Prize winner for national reporting, has covered the Summer Olympics for The Boston Globe *since 1976. He is the author of* Mary Lou, *the story of U.S. gymnast Mary Lou Retton.*

Summer Sanders, one of America's brightest new swimming hopes, won three medals at the 1991 Worlds, including the gold in the 200-meter butterfly.

Tamas Darnyi

If he were a country, Tamas Darnyi would have finished sixth in the men's standings at last year's World Championships. His three medals — two golds (and world records) in the 200 and 400 medleys and a bronze in the 200 butterfly— put Darnyi ahead of Australia, Canada, all of Asia and most of Europe. They also earned him 600,000 forints in bonuses from his home federation, roughly what a Hungarian worker makes in two years. But then, the 24-year-old Darnyi trains seven hours a day in a Budapest pool for one major meet every two years, and takes college courses in hotel management on the side. Darnyi won his two races in the 1988 Seoul Games by open water, setting world marks in each, and he'll be heavily favored to repeat at Barcelona. A childhood snowball fight left him virtually blind in one eye, but it hardly affects him in races. Anybody Darnyi might need to see is usually behind him.

the USA's "New Kids on the Block," a sprightly quintet of teenyboppers who were taking Driver's Ed. during the last Olympics.

And one of the strongest contenders for a 1992 gold medal wasn't even at Perth. Anita Nall, a 14-year-old from Maryland, came out of nowhere at last spring's U.S. Nationals to swim the second-fastest 200-meter breaststroke in history.

"There are people who don't believe in any barrier — whether it's a specific time or a name swimmer," says Reese. "That's what this sport fosters."

Stand still in swimming and you fall behind. There are no Nolan Ryans or Jimmy Connorses in chlorinated pools. Mark Spitz, who won a record seven gold medals at the 1972 Olympics, attempted a comeback last year at age 41. His times were barely good enough to win a junior championship.

The sport moves forward in a matter of hours, which is why nations seeking a demonstrable athletic impact often choose swimming. A rule change after the 1980 Olympics, limiting countries to two entries in each event (instead of three), has opened the way for smaller countries like Hungary, France and Italy to scoop up medals which previously would have gone to the U.S. or East Germany.

Biondi won seven medals for the U.S. at Seoul, and East Germany's Kristin Otto claimed six, all gold. Hungary brought only 11 swimmers (to the United States' 43) to the World Championships — yet won eight medals.

If a country is willing to invest the money and talent, it can develop a world-class swimming program in less than a decade. The Chinese didn't even make a final at the 1986 World Championships, but they earned four medals at the 1988 Olympics and six at Perth, four of them gold.

With only 21,000 registered swimmers (as compared to 180,000 in America), the Chinese have been labeled "The New Germans" — for both better and worse.

◆ HOW TO BUILD A DYNASTY ◆

The East Germans built a women's swimming dynasty in less than four years in the mid-1970s. For four Olympiads they ruled international swimming with aloof precision, turning up with paper-thin skinsuits, swollen shoulders, zipped lips and winning everything in sight. Later, several of the GDR's former swimmers and coaches admitted

Janet Evans

Janet Evans needed permission to skip school in 1988. Between races at Seoul, she still had to read <u>Ethan Frome</u> and <u>Siddhartha</u> and write an essay on Buddhism. Yet Evans still found time to squelch three different East Germans, win three gold medals and set one world and one Olympic record. Janet is 20 now and has put pounds and inches on what was a spindly 5'4" frame four years ago. She has also dropped out of Stanford and moved to Texas to spend more time preparing for the Games. This time Evans's rivals include not only Germans, but also China's Li Lin, Australia's Hayley Lewis and American teammate Summer Sanders. All of them beat her in the 400 medley at the 1991 Worlds, but Evans then was in the middle of her school year and off peak. Freed from her academic load, she will be favored to defend her titles in the 400 and 800 freestyles at Barcelona. This time, <u>Ethan Frome</u> stays home.

---

that illegal steroids had been an important part of their training.

The Chinese, who imported an East German coach to help set up their program, have the same goal the East Germans had: maximum medals with minimum bodies. They also use the same methods: hand-picked athletes (selected as young as age 6) who work together for much of the year, heavy state subsidies, advanced technical help from a national sports research institute (in Beijing), centrally trained coaches and performance bonuses equal to triple the average worker's salary.

So when the Chinese made some GDR-style progress at the 1990 Asian Games, rivals began hinting that they had been sampling East Germany's steroid stash, too.

A Hong Kong coach told *Swimming World* magazine that some of the Chinese women had "bulked up tremendously, some by 36 pounds, and their voices are very deep." A Canadian coach cocked an eyebrow at lickety-fast times and suggested that chemicals were the reason.

The Chinese, who, like the East Germans, have never had a swimmer test positive for drugs, insisted they were clean. "Let them spread the rumors," scoffed a team spokesman at Perth. "We know we are drug-free."

The Chinese women will make imposing ripples in Barcelona's Bernat Picornell pool. Zhuang Yong will be favored to win the 50-meter freestyle, Qian Hong the 100-meter butterfly. And Li Lin could sweep both the 200- and 400-meter individual medleys.

The Chinese are also just beginning to tap the potential of their billion people. "They have what the East Germans didn't — a much greater population base to deal with," says Mark Schubert, the U.S. women's coach.

For now, the Chinese are content to focus on the women's events, and only a few of those — the freestyle sprints, the butterfly, the individual medley. "That's how the East Germans did it at first, too," says Schubert. "But after a few years they got it all together. I'd be very surprised if the Chinese don't have people emerging in the other events before long."

◆ U.S. DEPTH ◆

Unlike most of their rivals, the Americans have always taken full teams to international meets. Last summer, they sent three different squads to the Pan Pacific meet in Canada, the Pan American Games in Cuba and the World University Games in England.

Few countries have the facilities or the talent reservoir to compete with the Americans across 31 races. So several, like Hungary, have targeted specific events and plucked medals from them. By focusing on the women's backstroke and the men's breaststroke and individual medley, the Hungarians won five gold medals at Perth and set three world records.

The Hungarian formula is simple — a hefty government subsidy (with generous bonuses for world or Olympic titles) for a small team which trains together year round in Budapest under an innovative coach (Tamas Szechy) who has 40 years' experience. "Hungary can get a few very talented athletes and take care of them well," says Schubert.

At the 1976 Games, American men won all but one of 13 races. In 1988, they won only five of 16, three of them relays. "We stood still and let people go by us," says Reese. "We just didn't improve — and the rest of the world did."

The rest of the world has been building 50-meter pools, pouring government money into training and sending their top people to U.S. universities to swim on scholarship against America's best. The results have been obvious. In the 1976 Games, only four nations won gold medals; in 1988, 10 did.

At Seoul, Krisztina Egerszegi, a 14-year-old Hungarian, won the 200-meter backstroke, which the Americans and East Germans had dominated for two decades. The Bulgarians went 1-2 in the women's 100 breaststroke, an East German plaything since the 1970s. And Anthony Nesty, whose native Surinam had only one Olympic-size pool, won the men's 100 butterfly, an event which America once owned, claiming eight of nine possible Olympic

World Records (as of 1/12/92)

Event		Men				Women		
Freestyle	50m	21.81	T. Jager	USA	1990	24.98	Y. Wenji	CHN	1988
	100m	48.42	M. Biondi	USA	1988	54.73r	K. Otto	GDR	1986
	200m	1:46.69	G. Lamberti	ITA	1989	1:57.55	H. Friedrich	GDR	1986
	400m	3:46.95*	U. Dassler	GDR	1988	4:03.85*	J. Evans	USA	1988
	800m					8:16.22	J. Evans	USA	1989
	1500m	14:50.36	J. Hoffmann	GER	1991				
Backstroke	100m	53.93r	J. Rouse	USA	1991	1:00.31	K. Egerszegi	HUN	1991
	200m	1:56.57	M. Zubero	ESP	1991	2:06.62	K. Egerszegi	HUN	1991
Breaststroke	100m	1:01.29	N. Rozsa	HUN	1991	1:07.91	S. Hoerner	GDR	1987
	200m	2:10.60	M. Barrowman	USA	1990	2:26.71*	S. Hoerner	GDR	1988
Butterfly	100m	52.84	P. Morales	USA	1986	57.93	M. Meagher	USA	1981
	200m	1:55.69	M. Stewart	USA	1991	2:05.97	M. Meagher	USA	1981
Medley	200m	1:59.36	T. Darnyi	HUN	1991	2:11.73	U. Geweniger	GDR	1981
	400m	4:12.36	T. Darnyi	HUN	1991	4:36.10	P. Schneider	GDR	1982
Freestyle relay	4x100m	3:16.53*	Jacobs, Dalbey, Jager, Biondi	USA	1988	3:40.57	Otto, Stellmach, Schulze, Friedrich	GDR	1986
	4x200m	7:12.51*	Dalbey, Cetlinski, Gjertsen, Biondi	USA	1988				
Medley relay	4x100m	3:36.93*	Berkoff, Schroeder, Biondi, Jacobs	USA	1988	4:03.69	Kleber, Gerasch, Geissler, Meineke	GDR	1984

* World record set at Olympics   r = performance in first leg of relay

The small but powerful Hungarian swimming team is particularly strong in the breaststroke, with such competitors as 100-meter world champion Norbert Rozsa.

Richard Martin / Allsport

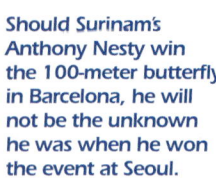

Should Surinam's Anthony Nesty win the 100-meter butterfly in Barcelona, he will not be the unknown he was when he won the event at Seoul.

medals between 1968 and 1976.

But few countries can dominate a stroke for long these days. In the 100 breaststroke, the fastest man was an American in 1984, a Canadian in 1986, a Briton in 1988, a Hungarian in the winter of 1991 and a Soviet last summer. "There's always someone who wants what you've got," says Reese.

Much of the sport's unpredictability has to do with its unique training cycles, in which swimmers peak for important meets by easing off heavy work loads (tapering) over several weeks, then shaving their bodies a day or so before they race.

◆ **CHOOSING THE TEAM** ◆

Countries which choose their teams by trials close to the Olympics, as the U.S. used to do, run the risk of having their swimmers go stale by "holding their taper" for another month or more. "In five or six weeks, you've got enough time to get tired but not enough to rest," says Reese.

That proved a problem in 1988, when the Americans held their team trials only six weeks before the Games. Since competition for spots was so fierce (world-record holders Pablo Morales and Steve Bentley didn't make the squad), nearly everyone had to taper and shave. But when they raced at Seoul, only a few swimmers posted faster times than they had at the U.S. trials.

This time the Americans chose their team in March, five months before the Games, giving the swimmers plenty of time to taper anew. The margins at the global meets have become too narrow to do otherwise.

At swimming's topmost aerie, the difference between first and last can be less than the length of an outstretched arm. At the world level, you can fit 10 swimmers into the span of one second. In the 100 butterfly at Seoul, Biondi misjudged the distance to the finish by a fraction and discovered that Nesty had touched him out for the gold medal.

◆ **A NEW BACKSTROKE RECORD ?** ◆

Although times are generally lowered in each successive Olympics, look particularly for faster backstroke performances — a consequence not just of stronger swimmers, but of rule changes.

When American David Berkoff revolutionized the backstroke at Seoul by swimming as much of the race as possible underwater, rules were developed to prevent it from happening again.

But the initial provision that a swimmer's toes

Nicole Haislett, one of the "New Kids on the Block" for the U.S., won the 100-meter freestyle at the 1991 World Championships.

break the surface within 10 meters has now been loosened to require the swimmer's head to surface within 15 meters.

This adjustment, in addition to a new stipulation freeing the backstroker from the requirement of a hand touch at the turn, should lower backstroke times considerably.

Most of the races at Barcelona will be too close for the television viewer — or even the officials on the scene — to call. Once judged by the naked eye and timed by hand-held stopwatches, swimming now relies on electronic touch pads (sensitive to a swimmer's fingertips) which calculate times to the hundredth of a second and register them instantaneously on a scoreboard.

Even at that, two American women (Nancy Hogshead and Carrie Steinseifer) had to share the 1984 gold medal in the 100 freestyle when they touched in the same heartbeat.

The 50 freestyle and the 100-meter races in each stroke frequently produce blanket finishes, with three or more swimmers touching together. If you're watching on television, focus on the middle lanes (3-4-5), where the fastest qualifiers from the morning heats are placed. More often than not, they will be the medalists.

But watch, too, for the "outside smoker," the swimmer in the outside lanes (1 and 8) who blows past the favorites in the final few meters. The swimmers in the middle lanes can't see the outside smoker through the thicket of thrashing arms and splashing water. That's how Australia's Hayley Lewis, barreling along in lane 8, knocked off the Americans to win the 1991 world title in the 200-meter freestyle.

The outside smoker can be almost anybody — the No. 2 swimmer from a strong country, a 14-year-old nobody knows, a college kid from Central America who has been swimming for the University of Florida. Count on at least one of them to upset the established world order at Barcelona. This year's New Kid on the Block could speak Danish.

Matt Biondi

Matt Biondi should have been long retired by now. "This is the last time you'll see me at a swimming race as a swimmer," he vowed in 1988, after winning seven medals in one Olympics. Biondi had planned to set off in his pickup truck to discover America and to swim with dolphins off the Bahamas. But restlessness and the lure of newly available prize money brought him back in time for last year's World Championships, where he won four medals, three of them gold. The most imposing swimmer in the world at 6'8", 210 pounds, Biondi may also be the most efficient. His smooth and seamless stroke makes him unbeatable in the 100 freestyle and the best relay anchor in the world. Biondi will be competing in his third Olympics at Barcelona, where he'll try to eclipse Mark Spitz's career record of 11 medals. After that? Perhaps water polo in 1996, the game Biondi loved most during his college days at Berkeley.

SYNCHRONIZED SWIMMING

By Barbie Ludovise

WOMEN
Solo
Duet

At first glance, it looks like a dance through watery aqua-blue. Costumed swimmers glide gracefully with the music, performing ballet-like movements above and below the water. All seems effortless. Everyone is smiling.

But don't let the smiles — or the sequined bathing suits — fool you. Synchronized swimming is not a prissy pastime but a demanding sport that requires not only grace and finesse but strength, skill and endurance.

An Olympic sport since 1984, synchronized swimming has worked to divorce itself from the la-di-da image of water ballet, popularized by Esther Williams and her band of bathing beauties in the 1950s. One only has to study "synchro," as it's often called, for a few moments to realize the challenges it poses.

Imagine performing a variety of gymnastic moves, such as splits, handstands or front walkovers, with the waterline as your balance beam. Consider the strength and power it takes repeatedly to propel your body out of the water, all the while looking as graceful as can be.

And don't forget: Through approximately 75 percent of your routine, you'll be holding your breath underwater. Passing out in mid-routine is not altogether uncommon.

At Barcelona, synchronized swimmers will compete in one or both of the two events: The solo competition features individual swimmers performing a 3½-minute routine in synchronization with music; in the duet, swimmers move in sync with each other and the music for a 4-minute period.

Judges award swimmers two separate scores ranging from 0 to 10, with one-tenth point increments. The first score is for technical merit: execution of strokes and figures; precision of patterns; synchronization with the music and, in duet, with the partner; and the degree of difficulty within the routine. The second score is for artistic impression: creativity and variety in the choreography, interpretation of the music and the manner of presentation.

All swimmers also must perform in the compulsory figure competition, which counts for 50 percent of their final score. This competition tests each participant's balance, flexibility and timing as well as her ability to control movement while executing four randomly selected figures out of a possible 28.

Like gymnastics and figure skating, synchronized swimming calls for a blend of athletics and aesthetics. Because appearance counts, unofficially that is, a new waterproof hairspray will be used instead of the traditional Knox gelatin to keep hair in place, as well as a custom-fitted nose piece to replace the standard look of the not-so-hip nose clip.

The United States and Canada have been leaders in the sport, though the Japanese and former Soviets are showing tremendous improvement.

Barbie Ludovise has been covering sports for the Los Angeles Times *for the last four years.*

1991 world champions Karen and Sarah Josephson would like to add an Olympic gold to the silver medal they won in the 1988 Games.

Kristen Babb-Sprague of the U.S. manages to project her elegance and grace even when upside down.

Kristen Babb-Sprague of the U.S., whom some compare to Olympic figure skating great Katarina Witt for her charisma and ability to connect with the audience, is among the favorites in the solo event. If she is to win the gold, she will have to defeat Canadian Sylvie Frechette, who has traded victories with her in recent years. Japan's Mikako Kotani, Olga Sedakova of the C.I.S. and Karine Schuler of France are also strong challengers.

Identical twins from the U.S., Karen and Sarah Josephson are the favorites in the duet competition. The Josephsons, or "the Js," as they're called, won the silver medal in the 1988 Olympic Games and then retired. After a year off, they returned to competition in 1990 and won every major competition they entered, including last year's World Championships.

"I've never witnessed two people swimming together with such a total mastery in all categories," said U.S. National Coach Charlotte Davis. "And perhaps because they're twins, their synchronization is tremendous. It's like watching a mirror image of each other."

The Josephsons came out of retirement because they wanted another shot at the gold medal. This will be their final chance, at least in the duet competition. At the 1996 Games, the solo and duet events will be replaced by a team competition, featuring eight swimmers performing simultaneously.

Currently, each nation may enter a total of just three swimmers. The change, many say, will draw more athletes — and more interest — to a sport that asks you both to sync and to swim at the same time.

TENNIS

By John Weyler

MEN
Singles
Doubles

WOMEN
Singles
Doubles

Sweden's Stefan Edberg would like to improve upon his performance in Seoul, where he tied for the bronze medal.

Most of the athletes in Barcelona's Olympic Village will have spent much of their lives training for a few minutes of competition with an Olympic medal on the line.

And then there are the tennis players. While kayakers, pentathletes, boxers, canoeists and team handball players were sweating in obscurity, driven only by the dream of someday standing on the highest level of the Olympic victory stand wearing a gold-plated piece of silver worth $105, some of the tennis players were trading ground strokes in an exhibition for a quick $100,000.

"For four years, their goal is the Olympics," says Chris Evert, who competed for the United States in the 1988 Summer Games in Seoul, Korea. "Oh, they have their other meets, but all their training is essentially for the Olympics.

"It's different with us. We have Wimbledon and the U.S. and French Opens, and we have to get pumped up for those. The other athletes are hungry for this, and I wonder just how many of the tennis players are really that hungry."

A lot of them, accustomed to luxury hotel, room-service cuisine, were probably hungry for some gourmet fare, while having to settle for the Olympic Village cafeteria. And some weren't exactly models of intensity when they hit the Olympic tennis courts at Seoul.

After a 60-year hiatus, tennis returned to the Olympics as a demonstration sport in 1984, then became a medal sport in 1988. The ideal of the Olympic experience became somewhat tarnished in the process.

In 1988, Soviet teenager Natalia Zvereva said she was very excited about coming to Seoul "because Olga [Morozova, her coach] said there were very nice leather clothes" in the city's shopping district.

Monica Seles, who at 17 won the 1991 U.S. Open, thought tennis wasn't "an appropriate" sport for the Olympics until a trip to Australia that year. She saw the swimming World Championships in Perth, became the youngest female to win the

---

John Weyler has been covering sports for the Orange County edition of the Los Angeles Times *since 1968.*

Australian Open and then announced she had decided to compete in Barcelona... if there was enough room for her racquet among the autograph books in her suitcase.

"After seeing the swimming and meeting [Janet] Evans and [Matt] Biondi, I thought, maybe if I go there I can meet all my idols, like in track and field," Seles said. "I have a long list of idols." (Her interest in idols notwithstanding, however, Seles was declared ineligible for her refusal to make herself available for Federation Cup play.)

And in some cases, this cavalier attitude spilled over into the competition. In the 1984 Games, having lost to unheralded Paolo Cane of Italy, second-seed Pat Cash of Australia commented that being upset by someone who wasn't ranked in the top 350

Only 16, Jennifer Capriati of the U.S. has already beaten some of the world's best women players. Her powerful ground strokes took her to the finals of the 1991 U.S. Open.

American Jim Courier, with his trademark white cap, served notice he had finally arrived when he won the clay-court French Open in 1991 and lost in the finals of the U.S. Open to Stefan Edberg.

players was "not the end of the world."

"This was a good chance for me to come to the Olympics, play some matches and see everything," Cash said. "I'm not getting a cent out of this, but I wanted to see the Olympics."

Tennis was only a demonstration sport in '84, of course, and Cash, a Wimbledon semifinalist that year, did add that he would have been more upset about losing if there had been a medal at stake.

Lackadaisical and sometimes even whimsical play continued in Seoul, however. There were gold, silver and bronze rewards for the winners, but Horst Skoff of Austria pulled a stunt usually reserved for practice matches. Rushing the net after hitting an approach shot, he then volleyed Stefan Edberg's return with a soccer header.

Would anyone try that at Wimbledon? Probably not. Would one ever play there, having done that? Definitely not.

But Stan Smith, director of coaching for the U.S. Tennis Association's player-development program, thinks the days are over of tennis players agreeing to play in the Olympics just so they can get an autograph or sneak in to see the men's basketball finals.

"My guess would be that the players will be taking it much more seriously this time than they did last time," Smith says. "I don't think they realized the enormity of the occasion as much as they should have."

> *"The Olympics, by their very dimension, humble anybody.... It's not a duplication of the grand slams."*

Tim Mayotte, who won a silver medal for the U.S. in 1988, admitted he initially was more intrigued by the notion of watching some of the other competition than by playing tennis. But it wasn't long before he was overcome by a tidal wave of Olympic spirit.

"I was excited beforehand, but after walking into that stadium for the opening ceremonies, I can't believe anyone would turn this down," he said before the tennis competition began.

Then, during fellow American Brad Gilbert's matches, Mayotte discovered the special feeling that comes from rooting for a teammate. "In tennis, your whole career is me, me, me," he said. "It spins on top of itself and it gets kind of empty after a while. The Olympics have inspired me to go out and try to play with a positive attitude.

"On the [professional] tour, sometimes you just get involved in all the money, the computer points and the rankings. This is totally different. It's really a breath of fresh air."

Czechoslovakia's Miloslav Mecir, who beat Mayotte to win the gold medal in Seoul, also said he gained inspiration from fellow athletes who were competing with a special gusto: "I feel something different in this event. You see the other sportsmen fighting for a place in history. You don't see that at other tournaments."

Former International Tennis Federation President Philippe Chatrier was the force behind

Germany's Steffi Graf hopes to duplicate the gold medal she won at Seoul.

The U.S. doubles team of Ken Flach and Robert Seguso won the gold medal at Seoul in 1988.

Last year Michael Stich broke through to his first major title win when he upset fellow German Boris Becker at Wimbledon.

tennis's inclusion as a medal sport in the Olympics after the 64-year gap, which had started with a rift between the International Olympic Committee and the ITF in 1924. ITF officials at the Paris Games complained about the lack of fully qualified officials, the absence of changing facilities and the sparse seating for spectators. When they were refused any say in future Olympic planning, the ITF withdrew from the Games.

During his campaign of more than a decade to get the sport back in the Olympics, Chatrier had always counted on the fact that even the millionaires of tennis would respond to the spirit of the Games.

"The Olympics, by their very dimension, humble anybody, any stars," he said. "It's not a duplication of the grand slams."

Part of the humbling process will surely be Barcelona's red-clay courts, whose slow surface is difficult for many of today's best players. Michael Chang of the U.S., who won the French Open on red clay in Paris as a 17-year-old in 1989, says tennis on clay becomes a "thinking man's game": One "can't just blast the ball all over the place and expect to win."

Big first serves bite into the rough surface and sit up for easier returns. Serve-and-volley players come to the net only to watch opponents run down their shots and come up with more chances to hit passing shots. Even power ground-strokers, who stay at the baseline, are forced into long rallies that test both their endurance and ability to avoid unforced errors.

The surface will definitely favor the clay-court specialists, such as (surprise, surprise) Spain's Sergio Bruguera, Emilio Sanchez and Arantxa Sanchez Vicario.

"Right now, you'd have to say the Spanish look pretty good playing at home on that surface," says Tom Gorman, captain of the U.S. Davis Cup squad and coach of the U.S. men's team in the 1988 Olympics.

A Spaniard in any of the medal rounds would surely change the popularity of the tennis competition, which did not even sell out for the finals in Seoul. But Spain's national favorites will have to wade through a draw that will include many of the top players in the world.

Each country will be represented by as many as three singles players of each sex — there are two guaranteed berths and a possible wild-card spot — and one doubles team in both the men's and women's draws. ITF eligibility rules state that all players must have been "available" to play in either the Davis Cup (men) or Federation Cup (women) for their countries in 1991. A player need not have actually competed in Cup play, but those who turned down an invitation to play probably would be disqualified by the ITF, as happened to Seles.

◆ SCHEDULING DIFFICULTIES ◆

The tennis competition in Barcelona runs from July 28 through August 8, which means it begins about three weeks after Wimbledon and ends about three weeks before the U.S. Open. Thus, it can present an enormous scheduling conflict for most players. A player wanting to compete in all three events first would have to prepare for and then play on grass at Wimbledon; practice and play on clay at the Olympics; and then train and compete on hard courts for the U.S. Open.

It would require a rigorous regimen, to say the least.

"A good clay-court player could stay in Europe after Wimbledon, play on clay and then go straight to Barcelona," said Smith. "But so much will depend on each individual's schedule. These players have lots of prior commitments."

Many of the top professionals' endorsement contracts require them to play in certain tournaments. Considering that Olympic rules will not allow advertisements on a player's uniform, it's possible some of the walking billboards of pro tennis won't be able to waggle a waiver from their shoe and clothing sponsors.

Even with all those problems, the stars figure to be out in force in '92. "I think the word has spread," said Gorman. "In '88, as the players spent time in the Olympic Village and watched the other sports, I saw the intensity grow on the tennis courts. In the 12 days of tennis, the event went from being like an exhibition to a big tournament. I think that will be the attitude of the players going in this time. They'll be treating it as a major tournament in Barcelona."

Tennis players can now share in the dreams of Olympic glory.

Most of the world's top-ranked women plan to make this battle for medals instead of money a memorable one. Steffi Graf, who ran on the Olympic Village track with the German track team and then beat Argentina's Gabriela Sabatini to win the gold medal in '88, became the first tennis player to win what is now known as the Golden Slam (Wimbledon, the U.S., Australian and French Opens, plus the Olympics).

Graf, who said she really enjoyed the privacy and quiet time she experienced in the Olympic Village in 1988, intends to play in Barcelona.

The men's field figures to include Edberg, Germany's Boris Becker and Michael Stich and a number of lesser-ranked players who might make an impact on clay courts. Among those could be France's Henri Leconte and Guy Forget, Austria's Thomas Muster and Andrei Chesnokov of the C.I.S., where tennis has enjoyed a boom in popularity since its return to the Olympics.

Arantxa Sanchez Vicario of Spain is particularly effective on a clay surface, with her strong baseline game and unrelenting ground strokes.

Several factors are involved in deciding who represents the U.S. in Barcelona. The selection process for the three singles nominees and the doubles team berths is based on eligibility, willingness to play and computer ranking.

"It's not like Davis Cup, where you can just pick the best players for the surface," Gorman said. "Our American procedures require us to go strictly by the rankings of the players who are eligible and want to play."

Jim Courier, winner of the 1991 clay-court French Open, and Chang might be considered the best candidates to compete for the U.S. on a clay surface, but they might not be the top two U.S. men in the rankings. Mayotte says he would compete again "in a heartbeat." Gilbert, who won a bronze medal in 1988, Pete Sampras and David Wheaton are also willing.

For the women, teenage sensation Jennifer Capriati, Mary Joe Fernandez and Zina Garrison are at once eligible — having competed for the U.S. in Federation Cup play in 1991 — and interested.

That seems to be the biggest difference in the attitude toward Olympic tennis since the first demonstration match in Los Angeles eight years ago. In most cases, the world's best players are eager to be a part of the Olympic tradition. Eager to put it all on the line in the name of country and sport.

"I don't think there are any more questions in the minds of the players about the importance of Olympic tennis," said Ron Woods, USTA director of player development. "There's a new wave of young players, and I think they all feel like tennis is really a part of the Olympics."

Some of the veterans may be just beginning to feel that way. Others, however, embraced the Olympic ideal from the very outset. On the same day in 1984 that Cash was downplaying the importance of his first-round loss, American Jimmy Arias was celebrating a victory with this testimony to the Games: "It has always been every athlete's dream to play in the Olympics, except tennis players. Now, this is a dream for us, too."

Michael Chang has been one of America's steadier performers for several years. His 1989 French Open championship on clay makes him a prime candidate for the U.S. team.

93

VOLLEYBALL
By Jonathan Lee

MEN'S EVENT
WOMEN'S EVENT

Craig Buck, a veteran of the 1984 and 1988 U.S. gold-medal teams, is one of the returning players on whom American hopes rest for a third consecutive Olympic title.

Half million dollar salaries for players, TV coverage three nights a week, Olympic gold medals dangling from American necks — what's happened to volleyball, the sport we used to play at picnics in the park?

The changes in volleyball in the last decade have been nothing short of revolutionary. The sport that was once a well-kept California secret is out of the bag, on the air and in the bank.

In 1991, Karch Kiraly and Steve Timmons, veterans of the '84 and '88 gold-medal U.S. teams, completed a five-month season in the Italian pro league, and each earned $500,000 for his efforts. They also won the championship and will be back next season at double the salary.

Though the commercial face of volleyball has been totally lifted, some things remain the same. The net is still 7'11 ⅝" for men and 7'4 ½" for women, and the court is still 30-feet square on each side. You can only touch the ball three times on your side, not counting touches by the blockers; you play three out of five games to 15 points; you need to win by two and can only score when serving — except in the fifth game of matches, when the receiving team can score as well.

But beyond those basics, the complexity and strategy of today's game bear little resemblance to the sport of yesteryear. It was the insight of Doug Beal, the 1984 U.S. Olympic men's coach, that transformed the sport and spawned the "new look" in indoor volleyball. What he devised, his team mastered, resulting in Olympic gold and imitation by the rest of the world's powers.

Volleyball in the 1980s: an age of specialization.

Instead of employing five players to receive the serve as had previously been done, he developed an innovative two-man formation. Why, reasoned Beal, spend thousands of hours of practice time, training a 6'8" middle blocker to pass, when you already possess smaller, quicker players with that skill? Under Beal's strategy, the big men stopped trying — with limited success — to handle the serve and took instead to the corners, ready to break into attack patterns, leaving the passing to Kiraly and Aldis Berzins, who received every serve... perfectly.

If the C.I.S. is to challenge for the gold, much will depend on the performance of Yuri Cherednik, their powerful striker.

The setter, Dusty Dvorak, took their consistently flawless passes and quarterbacked an efficient powerhouse offense. The passing problems of earlier American teams became history. From having failed ever to qualify for the Games, the U.S. won a gold medal in 1984, and the sport of volleyball took on a totally new appearance.

An age of specialization began. Big bangers got so good that they could crush the ball, even when they had to start their attack from the back row. With the likes of Timmons and Pat Powers pounding away, even the Soviets, Cubans and Brazilians were unable to stop the U.S. Over the next several years, some U.S. faces changed, but the tactics continued unchanged, and just as successful. And while every other team in the world tried to copy the U.S. style, the American personnel remained the absolute best.

Jonathan Lee, former editor of Volleyball *magazine, is a staff writer for* Volleyball Monthly. *He has traveled extensively in covering Olympic, World Cup and Pan Am Games volleyball competition.*

Cuba's strong and athletically talented squad is led by passer and swing man Lazaro Beltran (left) and setter Raul Diago.

Italy won the 1990 World Championship with players like 6'7" Andrea Zorzi, who had the benefit of playing in the Italian professional league under former U.S. Olympic Coach Doug Beal.

To disrupt the precision passing of the Americans, all of the top international players began using another new weapon — the jump serve. Players would throw the ball up, run, jump and fire away at the pair of passers in hopes of generating a service ace, or at least a bad pass.

It then became all the more important for teams to have two or three, not just good, but excellent serve receivers to harness the power of the jump servers. Their capacity to deliver accurate passes enabled the setters to prepare the big hitters with shots they could pound over the net for winners.

Today every team in the world uses these tactics, adjusting them to the particular skills of their players. Barcelona will exhibit them in all their variety.

Of the 12 teams comprising the Olympic pool, 10 were early qualifiers: The U.S., Italy, Spain, Canada, Japan, Algeria, the C.I.S., Cuba, Brazil and South Korea.

The U.S., with back-to-back Olympic gold medals in '84 and '88, would be top pick to do it again were it not for that old American value, capitalism. Many of the players responsible for America's success in the last two Olympics decided to see what they could earn if they hawked their skills on the open market. Several years and several million dollars in salaries later, it was clear the sale was a success. But what about the national team that the free enterprisers left behind?

The once proud USA jerseys began to be seen in consolation brackets of international tournaments instead of on award platforms. The talented new players could not keep up the gold-medal standards that Kiraly, Timmons, Bob Ctvrtlik, Craig Buck, Jeff Stork and company had set. America's success in defending its Olympic title in Barcelona may now rest on how many of those former players, who have been winning glory and lots of money in the Italian pro league, will return for another Olympics. Stork, the setter, and Buck, the 6'8" middle blocker are committed to rejoin the team. New head coach Fred Sturm has left the door open for the others to come back, an event which would bring instant credibility to the U.S. team and quite a bit of drama back to the 1992 Olympic stage.

But the return of the American golden boys will not guarantee anything. The rest of the volleyball world has grown, and grown and grown, especially teams from Italy, Cuba and the C.I.S.

◆ **THE PROFESSIONAL ITALIANS** ◆

In Italy, volleyball is the nation's number three sport, after soccer and basketball. The professional league has attracted top players for over a decade, providing the Italians with the opportunity to compete with and against the world's best talent. They won the World Championship in 1990 with stars of the lucrative pro league who were given time off to play at the World Championships.

Everyone from Italy's world champion team is expected to play in Barcelona. Featured in the Italian cast is veteran captain Andrea Lucchetta, who is the on-court team leader. Andrea Zorzi, however, leads the team in talent and potential. At 6'7" he's big on the right side at the net and hugely powerful on the right from the back row. Zorzi has just concluded a season playing for Beal, who, like many of his former players, left America for a generous Italian contract. How much he taught Zorzi and the rest could well determine Barcelona's finishing order.

◆ **CUBAN JUMPING ABILITY** ◆

The strength of the Cubans has always been gravity defiance. If you cannot manage a vertical jump of 40 inches, you need not apply for the team. This makes them a favorite of international volleyball crowds. If you like to watch slam dunk contests, rocket launches and human hovercraft, you'll love the Cubans.

The key player on the Cuban team is 6'3" Lazaro Beltran, a passer and swing hitter. According to U.S. assistant coach Jim Coleman, "Beltran is the best all-around player on the team. He's chubby, and not too tall, but he plays with his feet and his head and is just incredible." Beltran is joined by the team's veteran leader, Joel Despaigne, who, at only 25, has been a consistent performer in international circles for years. A tall dose of young talent is provided by 6'9", 19-year-old middle hitter Ihosvany Hernandez.

The Cubans have traditionally been weak in the setting position. But they have finally found Raul Diago, a steady, level-headed setter who can feed the

American medal chances in Barcelona will be vastly improved if Karch Kiraly, arguably the world's best player, returns from the Italian professional league.

Irina Smirnova, a reliable hitter for the C.I.S., attempts to block a spike by Caren Kemner of the U.S.

hitters. Now it is only their ability to play five full games at their peak that is in question. The current starters have been together for five years, and it takes a very solid effort to beat them.

◆ COMMONWEALTH ASPIRATIONS ◆

The C.I.S. plans a return to the glory years of the late '70s and early '80s, before the upstart Americans rained on the Soviet parade. They have enlisted Vyacheslav Platonov, who coached them throughout that period, and provided him with an imposing crew of physical specimens to make a gold medal a real possibility.

They have a dozen players between 6'7" and 6'9" who can all patrol the net with authority. Yuri Cherednik is their most powerful hit man, while Andrei Kuznetsov, a veteran of the Seoul silver-medal finish, adds experience to a talented, young team.

As big as the C.I.S. squad is, Holland dwarfs all others. With three players at about 7 feet and a 6'8" setter, they have a good shot at qualifying. They will contend with established powers Bulgaria and France and a united Germany, which has yet to unveil its new-look lineup, as well as a strong team from Argentina.

THE WOMEN'S COMPETITION

Eight women's teams will compete in Barcelona. Spain fills one of those berths by virtue of its host role, though its team will probably be among the weaker ones. But that is where the weakness ends. The remaining seven slots will be filled by squads of talent and depth.

Strategically, the women do not adhere to the U.S. formula as strictly as do the men. Many teams favor simplicity in their offenses, highlighting those individuals who have exceptional talent.

The former Soviets will participate as the defending Olympic champions, and have the size and experience to repeat. One resource they will

Wu Dan is one of the hardworking, efficient players who makes the Chinese a genuine threat for the gold medal.

Mireya Luis's jumping ability makes her a formidable presence at the net for the Cubans.

miss, however, is their gifted setter Irina Parkhomchuk, who just retired after 14 years. Their best defensive player, she also conspired with Valentina Ogienko, a 6'1" middle blocker, to outmaneuver and outblast the other world powers. The C.I.S. will need to find an able replacement to feed its strong hitters, 6'3" Irina Smirnova and 6'3" Tatiana Sidorenko.

◆ CHINESE DEFENSE AND CUBAN POWER ◆

China, gold medalist in '84, is very possibly the best in the world again. The Chinese earned their Olympic berth as runners-up in the 1990 World Championship to the U.S.S.R., and their eight-hour-a-day practices have only made them improve. Lacking great height, they are complete, all-around players, who play defense as well as offense. They are led by left-side hitter Xu Xin, who is only 5'8", but has a variety of shots, a powerful arm, and defends with the same tenacity that characterizes the entire Chinese team. Ma Fang, a 5'6" setter, is perhaps the world's best. China plays a business-like game, showing little emotion and simply executing its assigned tasks perfectly, but without the frenzy and peaks and valleys that most teams display. It works for them.

Cuba and the U.S. are two North American squads who will likely face off in Barcelona. The Cubans are an established world power, while the Americans are a team on the rise. Cuba's women are a corps of gifted athletes, who are perhaps the most graceful and impressive in the world. The Cuban setting is neither quick nor spectacular. It offers no surprises, just "come on up and try to stop us." Magaly Carvajal is the 6'3" middle hitter who gets high sets in the middle. Ragina Bell is a heavy-handed lefty, and Mireya Luis has been recognized as one of the world's best for some time. Though only 5'9", Luis touches 11'2". That puts her way over the 7'4½" net and most earthbound blocks.

◆ THE DEDICATED U.S. WOMEN ◆

Throughout the late '80s, the Cubans beat the Americans like a drum, but those days are over. In fact, the Americans are showing every sign of entertaining realistic medal notions like the ones they had in 1980, before the Olympic boycott. Not only did they take the bronze at the World Championship in '91, but they also split four games with the Soviet Union in a U.S. exhibition tour.

A dedicated group of athletes every bit as talented as the Cubans and hard working as the Chinese (well almost) accounts for America's upward mobility. Caren Kemner, a big asset for the U.S., is back in the lineup after knee surgery. Setter Lori Endicott runs a sweet offensive show that includes quickness, timing and outside firepower — the latter supplied by Kemner and Tara Cross-Battle. And a pair of sisters from California, Elaina and Kim Oden, are also accomplished hitters.

The rest of the women's pool consists of Japan, Brazil and Holland.

The 1992 Olympic volleyball competition is sure to be as dramatic as it is powerful. If you haven't seen the game at this international level, check it out. Then stand back. Even on TV it will be an explosive eyeful.

WATER POLO

By Michele Himmelberg Farmer

MEN'S EVENT

Seen from above, water polo can be as precise and rhythmic as a sailboat tacking into the wind, with players relying on timing, accuracy and swiftness.

What goes on below the surface, however, is more akin to an underwater rugby contest. With no pads for protection, only a nylon swimsuit and a head cap with ear guards, players fight vigorously for position, pushing, prodding, grabbing. The hips bump, the hands claw and the legs kick — sometimes for propulsion and sometimes for advantage. American Olympian Terry Schroeder recalls once having an opponent's entire foot in the back of his suit, driving him down in the water, while the opponent innocently held two hands in the air.

The object of the game is simple, and it's easy to follow the passing and shooting. A team of six field players attempts to score a point by putting a ball into a small goal, while they and their goalie strive to prevent the other team from doing the same. The goal measures three meters (9' 10") in width and one meter (3' 3") from the water up to the crossbar. A regulation pool is 20x30 meters and at least 1.8 meters (5'11") deep. Only goalies can touch pool bottom or grasp the ball with two hands. A player can shoot with any part of his body except the clenched fist. Players are not allowed to take the ball underwater, and a team must shoot within 35 seconds or lose the ball. The game is played in seven-minute quarters.

Strategy revolves around the hole man, or two-meter player, who stations himself two meters from the goal and acts like the pivot man in basketball. The other players fan out around him like an

A powerful hole man can shoot the wet, one-pound ball towards the goal at 50 miles per hour.

Allsport

100

umbrella. The hole man is the main scoring threat, and since he is under constant physical attack he may frequently draw a foul.

Fouling is an important part of the game. When an official calls an ordinary foul, a player has three seconds of "dead time" to put the ball back into play. Any violation during dead time results in a 20-second exclusion of the offender. Major fouls also require a 20-second exclusion, and they include

> *"When I took the shot, it felt like the whole team was trying to get the ball to go into the net."*
> *– TERRY SCHROEDER*

kicking, punching, submerging an opponent or dishonoring an official. The exclusion used to be 35 seconds, but was reduced in 1991 to speed up the game. Teams frequently score when they have a man advantage because of a foul.

Penalty throws are awarded when a player within four meters of the goal is fouled blatantly to prevent him from launching a shot on the goal. The penalty throws — or free shots, taken from the four-meter mark — are infrequent but important since major international games are often decided by a single goal.

Teamwork is critical for success in water polo. Regardless of the individual talent involved, the medal-winning teams are generally those veteran squads which play together as a single unit.

U.S. captain Terry Schroeder perhaps best evoked the importance of the team feeling when describing the last shot in the 1988 Olympic game between the U.S. and Hungary. With three seconds left in a tie game and each team needing a victory to advance to the final round, Schroeder recalls, "Everything suddenly seemed to go in slow motion. At that moment, you realize that if you don't score now, the four years of training you've put in goes down the tube, for you and everyone on the team. When I took the shot, it felt like the whole team was trying to get that ball to go in the net."

Schroeder's shot went in, leading the U.S. to its second-straight silver medal.

Michele Himmelberg Farmer covered the 1984 and 1988 Summer Olympics for the California Orange County Register, where she has been a columnist and sportswriter since 1983.

Returning captain Terry Schroeder will lead a U.S. team eager to trade in its last two silver medals for a gold.

The last two gold medals, however, have been won by Yugoslavia, and with a strong, experienced team — including excellent shooter Igor Milanovic — Yugoslavia could equal Great Britain's record of three straight golds, earned in 1908, 1912 and 1920 (there were no Games in 1916). It is unclear, however, what impact the internal strife in Yugoslavia could have on its Olympic teams.

The former Soviet Union also has had perennially top teams, and the host country, Spain, should be a contender with veteran Manuel Estiarte and his small but swift squad. Schroeder, hole man for the U.S., leads a team with a balanced attack and a premier goalie, Craig Wilson. The U.S. overtime victory against Yugoslavia to win the 1991 FINA Cup tournament suggests that the Americans will once again be strong contenders for the Olympic gold.

Water polo has been held in every Olympic program since 1900, making it and soccer the oldest team sports still played in the Games. Its elegance and underwater ferocity may not be limited to men for much longer: Women's water polo is under consideration to be added to the program, perhaps as an exhibition sport in 1996.

WRESTLING

By John Husar

MEN
FREESTYLE and
GRECO-ROMAN
up to 48kg/105.5 lbs
up to 52kg/114.5 lbs
up to 57kg/125.5 lbs
up to 62kg/136.5 lbs
up to 68kg/149.5 lbs
up to 74kg/163 lbs
up to 82kg/180.5 lbs
up to 90kg/198 lbs
up to 100kg/220 lbs
up to 130kg/286 lbs

U.S. freestyler Kenny Monday will be trying for a second consecutive 74kg gold at Barcelona. Here he defeats Soviet Adlan Varaev in the 1988 Games.

Mike Powell / Allsport

Don't look for the flashy bombast of a Hulk Hogan in the wrestling matches from Barcelona. Watch instead for sleek, wily foxes, for powerfully leveraged strategies, for the cat-like grace and stunning finality which characterize Olympic wrestling.

There are two distinct types of Olympic wrestling: freestyle and Greco-Roman. For most Americans, freestyle is the only form of amateur wrestling they know, the sport engaged in at the high school and college levels. Greco-Roman wrestling, practiced predominantly throughout Eastern Europe, differs from freestyle in that it does not permit holds below the hips.

With or without leg holds, however, wrestlers in both cases face each other on a mat and try to end the match quickly, or at least score as many points as possible within a five-minute period. Matches end in a "fall" when one man's shoulders are pinned to the mat for half a second. A "technical fall" occurs when a 15-point gap develops before time runs out.

John Husar, who covers Olympic wrestling for the Chicago Tribune, *writes regularly on sports and environmental issues.*

Otherwise, the match goes to the wrestler with the most points. In the event of a tie at the end of regulation time, an overtime period begins in which the first wrestler to score a point of any kind wins.

◆ **SCORING** ◆

There are three ways of scoring points — takedown, exposure and reversal. A takedown occurs when a wrestler forces his opponent to the mat, using any number of legal holds. This generally is worth one point, but can be worth more if the opponent is put onto his back. The referee and two judges signal appropriate numbers and the majority rules. A high amplitude takedown — a spectacular throw in which a man is hurled off his feet and through the air — can be worth five points.

Exposure, worth one point, occurs when a wrestler's shoulders are turned toward the mat, or in other words, if he comes dangerously close to being pinned. Another point can be earned by a reversal when a man fools or overpowers his opponent to move from beneath him to a controlling position on top of him. Points can pile up quickly when wrestlers are skillful and agile. At the same

time, great matches can also be low scoring as balanced opponents subtly vie for the one move that will win. Defensive specialists try to score early, then keep their opponents from making a successful move.

Wrestling's two styles have their own textures and rhythms, and athletes specialize in one or the other. Freestyle requires swift cunning and a bulldog's strength to reach inside an opponent, grab a leg or two and flip him over. Although Greco-Roman may seem strange to freestyle-bred Americans because of its prohibition on attacking an opponent's legs, it can be more dramatically overpowering. Great upper-body strength dominates, producing spectacular throws. Supported by cave drawings that go back 15,000 years, historians believe this kind of wrestling may be the oldest sport in the world.

At 62kg, John Smith, the first American wrestler with five world titles, exemplifies freestyle's classic strategy. He chips at opponents point by point with a maddeningly effective single-leg attack that bears his name. The "John Smith Single" resembles an attack of killer bees. Gifted with blurring hand speed, "John can do about 50 things with the single-leg attack," says a U.S. official. "And once he's in there, he plays off your defense. No matter how you react, there are five or six things he can do to make it worse for you."

◆ THE IMPLACABLE KARELIN ◆

On the other hand, at 6'3" and 130kg, super heavyweight Aleksandr Karelin of the C.I.S. epitomizes Greco-Roman's quest for total physical dominance. If he doesn't pin an opponent quickly, with his devastating reverse body slam, he piles up three-

John Smith of the U.S. (in red) defeated Soviet Stepan Sarkissian in 1988 for the 62kg title. If Sarkissian competes, Smith may well end up wrestling him again in the finals.

Aleksandr Karelin of the C.I.S. dominates super heavyweight Greco-Roman wrestling as few athletes have ever dominated a sport.

and five-point moves until the match ends when the maximum 15-point spread is reached. The challenge in wrestling Karelin is less to beat him than to try to score a point. He has already won a world title by blanking and pinning every opponent he faced.

Karelin's method is uncompromisingly brutal. Working from his knees above the prone opponent's hips, he scoops up his foe in a massive gut wrench, jerks to his feet, dips for leverage and wheels the man overhead to crunch him on the mat. Then he plasters him with his body — all in one smooth move. Opponents so fear Karelin's reverse lift that they try to escape it by wiggling around to face him. But then their backs are exposed and he merely has to tip them back to win by a fall. Men thus more or less give up rather than face the trauma of a Karelin fling.

The most feared wrestler in the world, Karelin has never lost a match in international competition. At the 1988 Olympics, he trailed Bulgaria's Rangel Gerovski by one point with less than 30 seconds to go in the final, but utilized his signature move to score a five-point takedown and secure the gold medal.

While Karelin remains the same unchanging force, the wrestling rules at Barcelona will not be exactly what they were at Seoul: International matches have been changed from two rounds of three minutes each to one of five minutes. Injury timeouts drop from three minutes to two. The complications of the four-point throw are gone; now all throws are worth five points. Also, to pep things up, wrestlers cautioned for passivity no longer resume in a disadvantaged position beneath their opponents, hoping only to hang on. They start face to face. In fact, passivity is severely discouraged: A wrestler can be disqualified for not wrestling hard enough. No one disqualified twice (Olympic wrestling is a double-elimination tournament) can receive a medal even if the second disqualification occurs in the finals.

◆ U.S. POSSIBILITIES ◆

Besides Smith, Americans who bear watching include freestyle world champions Zeke Jones (114.5kg) and Kevin Jackson (180.5kg); Kenny Monday, the 1988 Olympic and 1989 world champion at 74kg; and Bruce Baumgartner, a former Olympic and world champion super heavyweight. Baumgartner still has the quickness at 31 to bull inside for a double-leg takedown. He hopes to be the

first American wrestler to medal in three Olympics.

Barring injury, another U.S. hopeful is Chris Campbell, 37, a three-time World Cup champion at 90kg in the early '80s who started wrestling again after a five-year retirement. His comeback includes a silver at the '90 World Championships. A corporate attorney, Campbell takes his fax machine to training camps and wiles away his free time lawyering.

Internationally, strong freestylers include Korea's Kim Jong-Shin, who should dominate at 48kg, and a variety of wrestlers from the C.I.S.: Sergei Smal is the reigning world champion at 57kg; deceptively sleepy-looking, seven-time world titlist Arsen Fadzaev is back at 68kg; flamboyant Nasyr Gadzhikanov will test Monday at 74kg; and Makharbek Khadartsev, also an attorney, whose Cro-Magnon features have earned him the name of "The Rock," is a six-time world champion at 90kg. The Commonwealth features as well Leri Khabelov, who has won four World Championships at 100kg.

Although no medals are given for team competition, team scores are compiled on the basis of the first 10 finishers in each weight, and the U.S. urgently wants to achieve a freestyle victory over the former U.S.S.R. The last time this happened was in the 1960 Olympics when the U.S. came in second and the Soviets third. Since then the Soviets have always finished first. But with a better-funded national wrestling program permitting athletes to train year round and compete in important meets, the U.S. feels that Barcelona could witness the fulfillment of the American hopes.

In Greco-Roman, the U.S. will do well to finish fifth, well behind the Karelin-led Commonwealth. Only one American won a Greco-Roman medal in 1988, a bronze by Dennis Koslowski at 100kg. The best American hopes appear to be super heavyweight Matt Ghaffari and Shawn Sheldon at 52kg, each of whom won a silver at the 1991 World Championships. Hungary, Cuba, Germany and Yugoslavia also should do well.

Since 1983, Arsen Fadzaev of the C.I.S. (in red) has been a consistent international performer at 68kg.

OLYMPIC GOLD CHAMPIONS*
FOUR OR MORE GOLD MEDALS • 1896-1988

SPORT/Athlete	NATION	#	GAMES
ARCHERY			
Hubert Van Innis	BEL	6	'00, '20
ATHLETICS/TRACK			
Paavo Nurmi	FIN	9	'20-'28
Carl Lewis (2 in field)	USA	6	'84, '88
Alvin Kraenzlein	USA	4	'00
Melvin Sheppard	USA	4	'08, '12
Johannes Kolehmainen	FIN	4	'12, '20
Jesse Owens (1 in field)	USA	4	'36
Fannie Blankers-Koen	NED	4	'48
Harrison Dillard	USA	4	'48, '52
Emil Zatopek	TCH	4	'48, '52
Betty Cuthbert	AUS	4	'56, '64
Lasse Viren	FIN	4	'72, '76
Barbel Wockel	GDR	4	'76, '80
ATHLETICS/FIELD			
Ray Ewry	USA	8	'00-'08
Al Oerter	USA	4	'56-'68
CANOE/KAYAK			
Gert Fredriksson	SWE	6	'48-'60
Vladimir Morozov	URS	4	'64-'76
Ian Ferguson	NZL	4	'84, '88
DIVING			
Patricia McCormick	USA	4	'52, '56
Greg Louganis	USA	4	'84, '88
EQUESTRIAN			
Reiner Klimke	FRG	6	'64-'88
Hans Winkler	FRG	5	'56-'72
C.F. Pahud deMortanges	NED	4	'24-'32
Henri St. Cyr	SWE	4	'52, '56
FENCING			
Aladar Gerevich	HUN	7	'32-'60
Nedo Nadi	ITA	6	'12, '20
Pal Kovacs	HUN	6	'36-'60
Edoardo Mangiarotti	ITA	6	'36-'60
Rudolf Karpati	HUN	6	'48-'60
Ramon Fonst	CUB	4	'00, '04
Jeno Fuchs	HUN	4	'08, '12
Lucien Gaudin	FRA	4	'24, '28
Christian d'Oriola	FRA	4	'48-'56
Giuseppe Delfino	ITA	4	'52-'60
Carlo Pavesi	ITA	4	'52-'60
Gyozo Kulcsar	HUN	4	'64-'72
Yelena Novikova-Belova	URS	4	'68-'76

SPORT/Athlete	NATION	#	GAMES
FENCING (cont'd)			
Viktor Sidiak	URS	4	'68-'80
Viktor Krovopuskov	URS	4	'76, '80
GYMNASTICS			
Larissa Latynina	URS	9	'56-'64
Sawao Kato	JPN	8	'68-'76
Viktor Chukarin	URS	7	'52, '56
Boris Shakhlin	URS	7	'56-'64
Vera Caslavska	TCH	7	'64, '68
Nikolai Andrianov	URS	7	'72-'80
Akinori Nakayama	JPN	6	'68, '72
Agnes Keleti	HUN	5	'52, '56
Polina Astakhova	URS	5	'56-'64
Takashi Ono	JPN	5	'56-'64
Yukio Endo	JPN	5	'60-'68
Mitsuo Tsukahara	JPN	5	'68-'76
Nadia Comaneci	ROM	5	'76, '80
Nelli Kim	URS	5	'76, '80
Anton Heida	USA	4	'04
George Miez	SUI	4	'28, '36
Valentin Muratov	URS	4	'52, '56
Lyudmila Tourischeva	URS	4	'68-'76
Olga Korbut	URS	4	'72, '76
Ecaterina Szabo	ROM	4	'84
Vladimir Artemov	URS	4	'88
SHOOTING			
Morris Fisher	USA	5	'20, '24
Ole A. Lilloe-Olsen	NOR	5	'20, '24
SWIMMING			
Mark Spitz	USA	9	'68, '72
Matt Biondi	USA	6	'84, '88
Kristin Otto	GDR	6	'88
Johnny Weissmuller	USA	5	'24, '28
Don Schollander	USA	5	'64, '68
Charles Daniels	USA	4	'04, '08
Dawn Fraser	AUS	4	'56-'64
Murray Rose	AUS	4	'56, '60
Roland Matthes	GDR	4	'68, '72
Kornelia Ender	GDR	4	'76
John Naber	USA	4	'76
Vladimir Salnikov	URS	4	'80, '88
WATER POLO			
Paul Radmilovic (1 in swim.)	GBR	4	'08-'20
YACHTING			
Paul Elvstrom	DEN	4	'48-'60

*Includes discontinued events; excludes 1906.

Legend: ■ Men ■ Women

OLYMPIC COUNTRY CODES

Code	Country	Code	Country
AFG	Afghanistan	KOR	South Korea
AHO	Neth. Antilles	KSA	Saudi Arabia
ALB	Albania	KUW	Kuwait
ALG	Algeria	LAO	Laos
AND	Andorra	LAT	Latvia
ANG	Angola	LBA	Libya
ANT	Antigua	LBR	Liberia
ARG	Argentina	LES	Lesotho
ARU	Aruba	LIB	Lebanon
ASA	American Samoa	LIE	Liechtenstein
AUS	Australia	LIT	Lithuania
AUT	Austria	LUX	Luxembourg
BAH	Bahamas	MAD	Madagascar
BAN	Bangladesh	MAR	Morocco
BAR	Barbados	MAS	Malaysia
BEL	Belgium	MAW	Malawi
BEN	Benin	MDV	Maldives
BER	Bermuda	MEX	Mexico
BHU	Bhutan	MGL	Mongolia
BIZ	Belize	MLI	Mali
BOL	Bolivia	MLT	Malta
BOT	Botswana	MON	Monaco
BRA	Brazil	MOZ	Mozambique
BRN	Bahrain	MRI	Mauritius
BRU	Brunei	MTN	Mauritania
BUL	Bulgaria	MYA	Myanmar
BUR	Burkina Faso	NCA	Nicaragua
CAF	Central African Rep.	NED	Netherlands
CAN	Canada	NEP	Nepal
CAY	Cayman Islands	NGR	Nigeria
CGO	Peo. Rep. Congo	NIG	Niger
CHA	Chad	NOR	Norway
CHI	Chile	NZL	New Zealand
CHN	Peo. Rep. China	OMA	Oman
CIS	Comm. of Ind. States	PAK	Pakistan
CIV	Côte-d'Ivoire	PAN	Panama
CMR	Cameroon	PAR	Paraguay
COK	Cook Islands	PER	Peru
COL	Colombia	PHI	Philippines
CRC	Costa Rica	PNG	Papua N. Guinea
CUB	Cuba	POL	Poland
CYP	Cyprus	POR	Portugal
DEN	Denmark	PRK	DPR of Korea
DJI	Djibouti	PUR	Puerto Rico
DOM	Dominican Rep.	QAT	Qatar
ECU	Ecuador	ROM	Romania
EGY	Arab Rep. Egypt	RSA	South Africa
ESA	El Salvador	RWA	Rwanda
ESP	Spain	SAM	Western Samoa
EST	Estonia	SEN	Senegal
ETH	Ethiopia	SEY	Seychelles
FIJ	Fiji	SIN	Singapore
FIN	Finland	SLE	Sierra Leone
FRA	France	SMR	San Marino
FRG	West Germany	SOL	Solomon Islands
GAB	Gabon	SOM	Somalia
GAM	Gambia	SRI	Sri Lanka
GBR	Great Britain	SUD	Sudan
GDR	East Germany	SUI	Switzerland
GEQ	Equat. Guinea	SUR	Surinam
GER	Germany	SWE	Sweden
GHA	Ghana	SWZ	Swaziland
GRE	Greece	SYR	Syria
GRN	Grenada	TAN	Tanzania
GUA	Guatemala	TCH	Czechoslovakia
GUI	Guinea	TGA	Tonga
GUM	Guam	THA	Thailand
GUY	Guyana	TOG	Togo
HAI	Haiti	TPE	Chinese Taipei
HKG	Hong Kong	TRI	Trinidad/Tobago
HON	Honduras	TUN	Tunisia
HUN	Hungary	TUR	Turkey
INA	Indonesia	UAE	U. Arab Emirates
IND	India	UGA	Uganda
IRI	Islamic Rep. Iran	URS	Soviet Union
IRL	Ireland	URU	Uruguay
IRQ	Iraq	USA	United States
ISL	Iceland	VAN	Vanuatu
ISR	Israel	VEN	Venezuela
ISV	Virgin Islands	VIE	Vietnam
ITA	Italy	VIN	St. Vincent/Gren's.
IVB	British Virgin Is.	YEM	Yemen
JAM	Jamaica	YUG	Yugoslavia
JOR	Jordan	ZAI	Zaire
JPN	Japan	ZAM	Zambia
KEN	Kenya	ZIM	Zimbabwe

CONVERSION TABLES

cm. ⇌ in.			m. ⇌ ft.			km. ⇌ mi.			kg. ⇌ lbs.		
2.54	1	0.394	0.305	1	3.281	1.609	1	0.621	0.454	1	2.205
5.08	2	0.787	0.610	2	6.562	3.219	2	1.243	0.907	2	4.409
7.62	3	1.181	0.914	3	9.842	4.828	3	1.864	1.361	3	6.614
10.16	4	1.575	1.219	4	13.123	6.437	4	2.485	1.814	4	8.818
12.70	5	1.969	1.524	5	16.404	8.047	5	3.107	2.268	5	11.023
15.24	6	2.362	1.829	6	19.685	9.656	6	3.728	2.722	6	13.228
17.78	7	2.756	2.134	7	22.966	11.265	7	4.350	3.175	7	15.432
20.32	8	3.150	2.438	8	26.247	12.875	8	4.971	3.629	8	17.637
22.86	9	3.543	2.743	9	29.527	14.484	9	5.592	4.082	9	19.842
25.40	10	3.937	3.048	10	32.808	16.093	10	6.214	4.536	10	22.046

Use numbers 1 to 10 in center column to convert to or from the metric system.
For example: 5 cm. = 1.969 in.; 15 cm. = 3.937 in. + 1.969 in. = 5.906 in.; 100 m. = 328.08 ft.
8 in. = 20.32 cm.; 4 ft. = 1.219 m.; 150 lbs. = 45.36 kg. + 22.68 kg. = 68.04 kg.

OLYMPIC GOLD MEDALS • 1896-1988
INCLUDES ONLY EVENTS AT BARCELONA

	ARCHERY	ATHLETICS - TRACK	ATHLETICS - FIELD	BASKETBALL	BOXING	CANOE/KAYAK	CYCLING	DIVING	EQUESTRIAN	FENCING	FIELD HOCKEY	GYMNASTICS	JUDO	MOD. PENTATHLON	RHYTH. GYMNASTICS	ROWING	SHOOTING	SOCCER	SWIMMING	SYNCH. SWIMMING	TABLE TENNIS	TEAM HANDBALL	TENNIS	VOLLEYBALL	WATER POLO	WEIGHTLIFTING	WRESTLING	YACHTING	Total
USA	6	141	103	11	45	2	4	45	8			14				29	19		151	2			8	2	1	14	40	9	654
URS	1	27	37	4	14	28	10	4	6	18		72	5	5	1	12	11	2	12		4			7	2	39	62	3	386
GDR		21	18		5	14	6	2				6				30	3	1	38		1					1	2	2	150
ITA		10	3		14		20	3	6	31		11	1	2		8	6	1					2		5	6	1		130
HUN			8		9	6				31		11	8			5	3		14					6	2	16			119
GBR		28	7		12		1		5	1	3			1		16	4	3	12				10	4		3		4	114
FRA		6	3		3		19		10	28		1	3			2	4	1	1				2		1	9	3	3	99
SWE		4	7			9	3	4	17	2		2		9		2			3	1							27		94
JPN		1	3	1			1			27	12					1			14		3					2	20		85
FRG		6	9		2	5	5	3	16	8	1	1	1			8	5		4			1		1		2	2	3	82
FIN	1	23	13		2	2				6						3	3									1	26	1	81
AUS		14	3			3		2		1		3							36				1				1		64
GER*		1	5		2	1	2	8	1			9		1		9	1		6				1	1	4	3	1		56
ROM		3	6		1	8			1			13				7	5								2	7			53
TCH		5	4		3	4	2	1	1			11				2	3	1				1			3	1			42
POL		7	8		8			1	4			1	1			2	1					1			4	2			40
BUL		1	2		3	2				2						2	1		1							9	14		37
NED		4	1		1	7		5			1	1				4			9								1		35
CAN		6	2		3	3		1	1						1	3	4	1	6	2									33
SUI						1		4				14	1			4	1										4		29
YUG			1	3	2					5						1	2	1	1			3		3			4		26
NZL		7	1		1	5		2		1						3											4		24
TUR																								1		23			24
DEN			1		3	6	1		1							2	1		2								6		23
CUB		2	1		12					5			1										1						22
CHN						3		1				6					2				2		1	4					19
KOR	4			3							4							2	1							5			19
BEL		2			1	5	1	3		1						1	1							1					16
RSA		4	1		6		1										1					3							16
AUT			1			2			1	1		1	2				1							3					12
ARG		2			7											1		1											11
KEN		10			1																								11
NOR			2		1	1	1									1	2							1		1	1		11
MEX		3			2		1	2																					9
IND											8																		8
BRA		1	2										1											5	1		2		7
EGY																								1	5				6
EST*																													6
GRE		1			1			1		1						1									1				6
ETH		5																											5
ESP							1																	1	3				4
IRI																											4		4
IRL		2	2																										4
JAM		4																											4
MAR		3																											3
PAK											3																		3
POR		2																											2
PRK					1												1												2
URU																		2											2
BAH																											1		1
LUX		1																											1
PER																	1												1
SUR																			1										1
TRI		1																											1
TUN		1																											1
UGA		1																											1
VEN					1																								1
ZIM											1																		1
	12	360	252	16	168	96	96	70	98	137	19	214	34	27	2	150	93	19	318	4	4	9	26	14	20	116	281	46	2701

*Germany (GER), Estonia (EST) – medals prior to World War II

OLYMPIC GOLD MEDALS
BY NATION AND EVENT • 1896-1988

FINALS SCHEDULE†	1992	EVENT	1988	1984	1980	1976	1972	1968	1964	1960	1956	1952	1948	1936	1932	1928	1924	1920	1912	1908	1904	1900	1896
		ATHLETICS - TRACK																					
Sat - Aug 1 - 2:00 pm		100m	USA	USA	GBR	TRI	URS	USA	USA	FRG	USA	USA	USA	USA	USA	CAN	GBR	USA	USA	RSA	USA	USA	USA
Wed - Aug 5 - 2:50 pm		200m	USA	USA	ITA	JAM	URS	USA	ITA	USA	USA	USA	USA	USA	USA	CAN	GBR	USA	CAN	USA	USA		
Wed - Aug 5 - 2:20 pm		400m	USA	USA	URS	CUB	USA	USA	USA	USA	USA	JAM	JAM	USA	USA	USA	GBR	RSA	USA	GBR	USA	USA	
Sat - Aug 8 - 1:20 pm		4 x 100m	URS	USA	URS	USA	USA	USA	USA	FRG	USA	USA	USA	USA	USA	USA	USA	GBR					
Sat - Aug 8 - 3:40 pm		4 x 400m	USA	USA	URS	USA	KEN	USA	USA	USA	JAM	USA	USA	GBR	USA	USA	USA	GBR	USA	USA*			
Wed - Aug 5 - 3:05 pm		800m	KEN	BRA	GBR	CUB	USA	AUS	NZL	NZL	USA	USA	USA	USA	GBR	GBR	GBR	GBR	USA	USA	USA	GBR	AUS
Sat - Aug 8 - 2:15 pm		1500m	KEN	GBR	GBR	NZL	FIN	KEN	NZL	AUS	IRL	LUX	SWE	NZL	ITA	FIN	FIN	GBR	GBR	USA	USA	GBR	AUS
Sat - Aug 8 - 2:40 pm		5,000m	KEN	MAR	ETH	FIN	FIN	TUN	USA	NZL	URS	TCH	BEL	FIN	FIN	FIN	FIN	FIN	FRA	FIN			
Mon - Aug 3 - 3:45 pm		10,000m	MAR	ITA	ETH	FIN	FIN	KEN	USA	URS	URS	TCH	TCH	FIN	POL	FIN	FIN	FIN	FIN				
Sun - Aug 9 - 12:30 pm		Marathon	ITA	POR	GDR	GDR	USA	ETH	ETH	ETH	FRA	TCH	ARG	JPN	ARG	FRA	FIN	FIN	RSA	USA	USA	FRA	GRE
Mon - Aug 3 - 2:05 pm		110m hurdles	USA	USA	GDR	FRA	USA	USA	USA	USA	USA	USA	USA	USA	USA	RSA	USA	CAN	USA	USA	USA	USA	USA
Thu - Aug 6 - 1:00 pm		400m hurdles	USA	USA	GDR	USA	UGA	GBR	USA	USA	USA	USA	USA	USA	IRL	GBR	USA	USA		USA	USA	USA	
Fri - Aug 7 - 3:00 pm		Steeplechase	KEN	KEN	POL	SWE	KEN	KEN	BEL	POL	GBR	USA	SWE	FIN	FIN	FIN	FIN	GBR		GBR*	USA*	CAN*/USA*	
Fri - July 31 - 1:15 pm		20 km walk	TCH	MEX	ITA	MEX	GDR	URS	GBR	URS	URS												
Fri - Aug 7 - 1:30 am		50 km walk	URS	MEX	GDR		FRG	GDR	ITA	GBR	NZL	ITA	SWE	GBR	GBR								
Sat - Aug 1 - 1:45 pm		100m	USA	USA	URS	FRG	GDR	USA	USA	USA	AUS	AUS	NED	USA	POL	USA							
Wed - Aug 5 - 2:35 pm		200m	USA	USA	GDR	GDR	GDR	POL	USA	USA	AUS	AUS	NED										
Thu - Aug 6 - 12:30 pm		400m	URS	USA	GDR	POL	GDR	FRA	AUS														
Sat - Aug 8 - 1:00 pm		4 x 100m	USA	USA	GDR	GDR	FRG	USA	POL	USA	AUS	USA	NED	USA	USA	CAN							
Sat - Aug 8 - 3:15 pm		4 x 400m	URS	USA	URS	GDR	GDR	GDR															
Sun - Aug 2 - 2:45 pm		800m	GDR	ROM	URS	URS	FRG	USA	GBR	URS						GER							
Sat - Aug 8 - 1:50 pm		1500m	ROM	ITA	URS	URS	URS																
Sun - Aug 2 - 3:00 pm		3,000m	URS	ROM																			
Fri - Aug 7 - 3:20 pm		10,000m	URS																				
Sat - Aug 1 - 12:30 pm		Marathon	POR	USA																			
Thu - Aug 6 - 2:10 pm		100m hurdles	BUL	USA	URS	GDR	GDR	AUS*	GDR*	URS*	AUS*	AUS*	NED*	ITA*	USA*								
Mon - Aug 3 - 3:30 pm		400m hurdles	AUS	MAR																			
Mon - Aug 3 - 1:50 pm		10 km walk																					
		ATHLETICS - FIELD																					
Sun - Aug 2 - 12 noon		High jump	URS	FRG	GDR	POL	URS	USA	URS	URS	USA	USA	AUS	USA	CAN	USA	USA	USA	USA	USA	USA	USA	USA
Fri - Aug 7 - 11:00 am		Pole vault	URS	FRA	POL	POL	GDR	USA	USA	USA	USA	USA	USA	USA	USA	USA	USA	USA	USA	USA	USA	USA	USA
Thu - Aug 6 - 12:50 pm		Long jump	USA	USA	GDR	USA	USA	USA	GBR	USA	USA	USA	USA	USA	USA	USA	USA	SWE	USA	USA	USA		
Mon - Aug 3 - 1:30 pm		Triple jump	BUL	USA	URS	URS	URS	URS	POL	POL	BRA	BRA	SWE	JPN	JPN	JPN	AUS	FIN	SWE	GBR	USA		
Fri - July 31 - 1:00 pm		Shot put	GDR	ITA	URS	GDR	POL	USA	USA	USA	USA	USA	USA	GER	USA	USA	USA	FIN	USA	USA	USA	USA	USA
Wed - Aug 5 - 1:30 pm		Discus	GDR	FRG	URS	USA	TCH	USA	USA	USA	USA	USA	ITA	USA	USA	USA	USA	FIN	FIN	USA	USA	HUN	USA
Sat - Aug 8 - 12:55 pm		Javelin	FIN	FIN	URS	HUN	FRG	URS	FIN	URS	NOR	USA	FIN	GER	FIN	SWE	FIN	FIN	SWE	SWE			
Sun - Aug 2 - 10:30 am		Hammer	URS	FIN	URS	URS	URS	HUN	URS	USA	HUN	HUN	HUN	GER	IRL	IRL	USA	USA	USA	USA	USA		
Thu - Aug 6 - 3:15 pm		Decathlon	GDR	GBR	GBR	USA	URS	USA	FRG	USA	USA	USA	USA	USA	USA	FIN	USA	NOR	SWE/USA				
Sat - Aug 8 - 12:30 pm		High jump	USA	FRG	ITA	GDR	FRG	TCH	ROM	ROM	USA	RSA	USA	HUN	USA	CAN							
Fri - Aug 7 - 1:15 pm		Long jump	USA	ROM	URS	GDR	FRG	ROM	GBR	URS	POL	NZL	HUN										
Fri - Aug 7 - 12:55 pm		Shot put	URS	FRG	GDR	BUL	URS	GDR	URS	URS	URS	TCH	FRA										
Mon - Aug 3 - 12:50 pm		Discus	GDR	NED	GDR	GDR	URS	ROM	URS	URS	TCH	URS	FRA	GER	USA	POL							
Sat - Aug 1 - 1:20 pm		Javelin	GDR	GBR	CUB	GDR	GDR	HUN	ROM	URS	URS	TCH	AUT	GER	USA								
Sun - Aug 2 - 3:30 pm		Heptathlon/Pentathlon	USA	AUS	URS	GDR	GBR	FRG	URS														
		BASEBALL																					
Wed - Aug 5 - 3:00pm		Men																					
		BASKETBALL																					
Sat - Aug 8 - 4:00 pm		Men	URS	USA	YUG	USA	URS	USA	USA	USA	USA	USA	USA										
Fri - Aug 7 - 4:00 pm		Women	USA	USA	URS	URS																	
		BOXING																					
Sat - Aug 8 - 4:00 am		48kg	BUL	USA	URS	CUB	HUN	VEN															
Sat - Aug 8 - 4:30 am		51kg	KOR	USA	BUL	USA	BUL	MEX	ITA	HUN	GBR	USA	ARG	GER	HUN	HUN	USA	USA		USA			
Sat - Aug 8 - 5:00 am		54kg	USA	ITA	CUB	PRK	CUB	URS	JPN	URS	FRG	FIN	HUN	ITA	CAN	ITA	RSA	RSA		GBR	USA		
Sat - Aug 8 - 5:30 am		57kg	ITA	USA	GDR	CUB	URS	MEX	URS	URS	URS	TCH	ARG	ARG	NED	USA	FRA		GBR	USA			
Sat - Aug 8 - 6:00 am		60kg	GDR	USA	CUB	USA	POL	USA	POL	POL	GBR	ITA	RSA	HUN	RSA	ITA	DEN	USA		GBR	USA		
Sat - Aug 8 - 6:30 am		63.5kg	URS	USA	ITA	USA	USA	POL	POL	TCH	URS	USA											
Sun - Aug 9 - 4:00 am		67kg	KEN	USA	CUB	GDR	CUB	GDR	POL	ITA	ROM	POL	TCH	FIN	USA	NZL	BEL	CAN		USA			
Sun - Aug 9 - 4:30 am		71kg	KOR	USA	CUB	POL	FRG	URS	URS	USA	HUN	HUN											
Sun - Aug 9 - 5:00 am		75kg	GDR	KOR	CUB	USA	URS	URS	URS	GBR	URS	URS	HUN	USA	FRA	USA	ITA	GBR		GBR	USA		
Sun - Aug 9 - 5:30 am		81kg	USA	YUG	YUG	USA	YUG	ITA	URS	URS	USA	USA	RSA	FRA	ARG	ARG	GBR	USA					
Sun - Aug 9 - 6:00 am		91kg	USA	USA																			
Sun - Aug 9 - 6:30 am		+91kg	CAN	USA	CUB	CUB	CUB	USA	USA	USA	USA	USA	ARG	GER	ARG	ARG	NOR	GBR		GBR	USA		
		DIVING																					
Tue - Aug 4 - 9:00 am		Platform	USA	USA	GDR	ITA	ITA	ITA	USA	USA	MEX	USA	USA	USA	USA	USA	USA	USA	SWE	SWE	USA*		
Wed - July 29 - 9:00 am		Springboard	USA	USA	URS	USA	USA	USA	USA	USA	USA	USA	USA	USA	USA	USA	USA	USA	GER	GER			
Mon - July 27 - 9:00 am		Platform	CHN	CHN	GDR	URS	SWE	TCH	USA	FRG	USA	USA	USA	USA	USA	USA	USA	USA	DEN	SWE			
Mon - Aug 3 - 8:30 am		Springboard	CHN	CAN	URS	USA	USA	USA	FRG	USA	USA	USA	USA	USA	USA	USA	USA	USA					
		EQUESTRIAN																					
Wed - Aug 5 - 3:00 am		Individual dressage	FRG	FRG	AUT	SUI	FRG	URS	SUI	URS	SWE	SWE	SUI	GER	FRA	GER	SWE	SWE	SWE				
Sun - Aug 9 - 7:30 am		Ind. show jumping	FRA	USA	POL	FRG	ITA	USA	FRA	ITA	FRG	FRA	MEX	GER	JPN	TCH	SUI	ITA	FRA			BEL	

‡ Time that finals occur (Eastern Daylight Saving Time). Some events may not be shown live on TripleCast. Event and broadcast schedules are as of 1/12/92 and are subject to change.

• For summary by nation and sport, see page 107.
* Differed slightly from current event.

■ Men ■ Women ■ Open

FINALS SCHEDULE‡	1992	EVENT	1988	1984	1980	1976	1972	1968	1964	1960	1956	1952	1948	1936	1932	1928	1924	1920	1912	1908	1904	1900	1896
Thu - July 30 - 11:00 am		Individual three day	NZL	NZL	ITA	USA	GBR	FRA	ITA	AUS	SWE	SWE	FRA	GER	NED	NED	NED	SWE	SWE				
Mon - Aug 3 - 10:00 am		Team dressage	FRG	FRG	URS	FRA	URS	FRG	FRG		SWE	SWE	FRA	GER	FRA	GER							
Tue - Aug 4 - 9:00 am		Team show jumping	FRG	USA	URS	FRA	FRG	CAN	FRG	FRG	GBR	MEX	GER		ESP	SWE	SWE	SWE					
Thu - July 30 - 11:00 am		Team three day	FRG	USA	URS	USA	GBR	GBR	ITA	AUS	GBR	SWE	USA	GER	USA	NED	NED	SWE	SWE				
		GYMNASTICS																					
Sun - Aug 2 - 2:00 pm		Floor exercise	URS	CHN	GDR	URS	URS	JPN	ITA	JPN	URS	SWE	HUN	SUI	HUN								
Sun - Aug 2 - 2:00 pm		High bar	URS/URS	JPN	BUL	JPN	JPN	JPN/URS	URS	JPN	JPN	SUI	SUI	FIN	USA	SUI	YUG			USA		GER	
Sun - Aug 2 - 2:00 pm		Pommel horse	URS BUL HUN	CHN USA	HUN	HUN	URS	YUG	YUG	URS FIN	URS	URS	FIN	GER	HUN	SUI	SUI			USA		SUI	
Sun - Aug 2 - 2:00 pm		Vault	CHN	CHN	URS	URS	GDR	URS	JPN	URS JPN	URS FRG	URS	FIN	GER	ITA	SUI	USA			USA		GER	
Sun - Aug 2 - 2:00 pm		Parallel bars	URS	USA	URS	JPN	JPN	JPN	URS	URS	SUI	SUI	GER	ITA	TCH	SUI				USA		GER	
Sun - Aug 2 - 2:00 pm		Rings	URS GDR	CHN JPN	URS	JPN	JPN	JPN	URS	URS	URS	SUI	TCH	USA	ITA					USA		GRE	
Fri - July 31 - 2:00 pm		All-around	URS	JPN	URS	JPN	JPN	JPN	JPN	URS	URS	URS	FIN	GER	ITA*	SUI*	YUG*	ITA*	ITA*	ITA*	AUT*	FRA*	
Wed - July 29 - 2:00 pm		Team competition	URS	USA	URS	JPN	JPN	JPN	JPN	JPN	URS	URS	FIN	GER	ITA*	SUI*	ITA*	ITA*	SWE*	USA*			
Sat - Aug 1 - 2:00 pm		Floor exercise	ROM	ROM	URS ROM	URS	URS	TCH	URS	URS	URS HUN	HUN											
Sat - Aug 1 - 2:00 pm		Uneven bars	ROM	USA CHN	GDR	ROM	GDR	TCH	URS	URS	HUN	HUN											
Sat - Aug 1 - 2:00 pm		Balance beam	ROM	ROM ROM	ROM	ROM	URS	URS	TCH	TCH	HUN	URS											
Sat - Aug 1 - 2:00 pm		Vault	URS	ROM	URS	URS	GDR	TCH	TCH	URS	URS												
Thu - July 30 - 2:00 pm		All-around	URS	USA	URS	ROM	URS	TCH	TCH	URS	URS	URS											
Tue - July 28 - 2:00 pm		Team competition	URS	ROM	URS	URS	URS	URS	URS	URS	URS*	URS*	TCH*	GER*		NED*							
		RHYTHMIC GYMNASTICS																					
Sat - Aug 8 - 10:00 am		All-around	URS	CAN																			
		SOCCER																					
Sat - Aug 8 - 2:00 pm		Men	URS	FRA	TCH	GDR	POL	HUN	HUN	YUG	URS	HUN	SWE	ITA		URU	URU	BEL	GBR	GBR	CAN	GBR	
		SWIMMING																					
Thu - July 30 - 12 noon		50m freestyle	USA															HUN					
Tue - July 28 - 12 noon		100m freestyle	USA	USA	GDR	USA	USA	AUS	USA	AUS	AUS	USA	USA	HUN	JPN	USA	USA	USA	USA	HUN*		HUN	
Sun - July 26 - 12 noon		200m freestyle	AUS	FRG	URS	USA	USA	AUS													USA*		AUS	
Wed - July 29 - 12 noon		400m freestyle	GDR	USA	URS	AUS	USA	USA	AUS	AUS	FRA	USA	USA	USA	ARG	USA	USA	CAN	GBR	USA*		AUT*	
Fri - July 31 - 12 noon		1500m freestyle	URS	USA	URS	USA	USA	USA	AUS	AUS	AUS	USA	USA	JPN	JPN	SWE	AUS	USA	CAN	GBR	GER*	GBR*	HUN*
Sun - July 26 - 12 noon		100m breaststroke	GBR	USA	GBR	USA	JPN	USA															
Wed - July 29 - 12 noon		200m breaststroke	HUN	CAN	URS	GBR	USA	MEX	AUS	USA	JPN	AUS	USA	JPN	JPN	USA	SWE	GER	GBR				
Mon - July 27 - 12 noon		100m butterfly	SUR	FRG	SWE	USA	USA	USA															
Thu - July 30 - 12 noon		200m butterfly	FRG	AUS	URS	USA	USA	USA	USA	AUS	USA	USA	USA	JPN	USA	USA	USA	GER	GER*				
Thu - July 30 - 12 noon		100m backstroke	JPN	USA	SWE	USA	GDR	GDR		AUS	AUS	USA	USA	USA	JPN	USA	USA	USA	USA	GER	GER*		
Tue - July 28 - 12 noon		200m backstroke	URS	USA	HUN	USA	GDR	GDR	USA												GER			
Fri - July 31 - 12 noon		200m ind. medley	HUN	CAN			SWE	USA															
Mon - July 27 - 12 noon		400m ind. medley	HUN	CAN	URS	USA	SWE	USA	USA														
Wed - July 29 - 12 noon		4x100m freestyle relay	USA	USA			USA	USA	USA														
Mon - July 27 - 12 noon		4x200m freestyle relay	USA	USA	URS	USA	USA	USA	USA	USA	AUS	USA	USA	JPN	USA	USA	USA	AUS	GBR				
Fri - July 31 - 12 noon		4x100m medley relay	USA	USA	AUS	USA	USA	USA	USA	USA													
Fri - July 31 - 12 noon		50m freestyle	GDR																				
Sun - July 26 - 12 noon		100m freestyle	GDR	USA USA	GDR	GDR	USA	USA	AUS	AUS	AUS	HUN	DEN	NED	USA	USA	USA	AUS					
Mon - July 27 - 12 noon		200m freestyle	GDR	USA	GDR	GDR	AUS	USA															
Tue - July 28 - 12 noon		400m freestyle	USA	USA	GDR	GDR	AUS	USA	USA	AUS	HUN	USA	NED	USA	USA	USA	USA*						
Thu - July 30 - 12 noon		800m freestyle	USA	USA	AUS	GDR	USA	USA															
Wed - July 29 - 12 noon		100m breaststroke	BUL	NED	GDR	GDR	USA	YUG															
Mon - July 27 - 12 noon		200m breaststroke	GDR	CAN	URS	URS	AUS	USA	URS	GBR	FRG	HUN	NED	JPN	AUS	GER	GBR						
Wed - July 29 - 12 noon		100m butterfly	GDR	USA	GDR	GDR	JPN	AUS	USA	USA													
Fri - July 31 - 12 noon		200m butterfly	GDR	USA	GDR	GDR	USA	NED															
Tue - July 28 - 12 noon		100m backstroke	GDR	USA	GDR	GDR	USA	USA	USA	GBR	RSA	DEN	NED	USA	NED	USA							
Fri - July 31 - 12 noon		200m backstroke	HUN	NED	GDR	GDR	USA	USA															
Thu - July 30 - 12 noon		200m ind. medley	GDR	USA			AUS	USA															
Sun - July 26 - 12 noon		400m ind. medley	USA	USA	GDR	GDR	AUS	USA	USA														
Tue - July 28 - 12 noon		4x100m freestyle relay	GDR	USA	GDR	USA	USA	USA	USA	AUS	HUN	USA	NED	USA	USA	USA	GBR						
Thu - July 30 - 12 noon		4x100m medley relay	GDR	USA	GDR	GDR	USA	USA	USA														
		SYNCHRONIZED SWIMMING																					
Thu - Aug 6 - 9:00 am		Solo	CAN	USA																			
Fri - Aug 7 - 9:00 am		Duet	CAN	USA																			
		TENNIS																					
Sat - Aug 8 - 8:00 am		Singles	TCH														USA	RSA	RSA	GBR	USA	GBR	GBR	
Fri - Aug 7 - 5:00 am		Doubles	USA														USA	GBR	RSA	GBR	USA	GBR	GBR GER	
Fri - Aug 7 - 8:00 am		Singles	FRG														USA	FRA	FRA	GBR		GBR		
Sat - Aug 8 - 5:00 am		Doubles	USA														USA	GBR						
		VOLLEYBALL																					
Sun - Aug 9 - 7:00 am		Men	USA	USA	URS	POL	JPN	URS	URS														
Fri - Aug 7 - 3:30 pm		Women	URS	CHN	URS	JPN	URS	URS	JPN														
		WATER POLO																					
Sun - Aug 9 - 10:30 am		Men	YUG	YUG	URS	HUN	URS	YUG	HUN	ITA	HUN	HUN	ITA	HUN	HUN	GER	FRA	GBR	GBR	GBR	USA	GBR	
		WRESTLING																					
Thu - Aug 6 - 1:00 pm		48kg freestyle	JPN	USA	ITA	BUL	URS														USA			
Wed - Aug 5 - 1:00 pm		52kg freestyle	JPN	YUG	URS	USA	JPN	JPN	JPN	TUR	URS	TUR	FIN								USA			
Fri - Aug 7 - 11:00 am		57kg freestyle	URS	JPN	URS	URS	JPN	JPN	JPN	USA	TUR	JPN	TUR	HUN*	USA*	FIN*	FIN*			USA*	USA*		

109

FINALS SCHEDULE‡	1992	EVENT	1988	1984	1980	1976	1972	1968	1964	1960	1956	1952	1948	1936	1932	1928	1924	1920	1912	1908	1904	1900	1896
Fri - Aug 7 - 11:00 am		62kg freestyle	USA	USA	URS	KOR	URS	JPN*	JPN*	TUR*	JPN*	TUR*	TUR*	FIN*	FIN*	USA*	USA*		USA*	USA*			
Wed - Aug 5 - 1:00 pm		68kg freestyle	URS	KOR	URS	URS	USA	IRI*	BUL*	USA*	IRI*	SWE*	TUR*	HUN*	FRA*	EST*	USA*	FIN*		GBR*	USA*			
Thu - Aug 6 - 1:00 pm		74kg freestyle	USA	USA	BUL	JPN	USA	TUR*	USA*	JPN*	USA*	TUR*	USA*	USA*	FIN*	SUI*					USA*			
Fri - Aug 7 - 11:00 am		82kg freestyle	KOR	USA	BUL	USA	URS	URS*	BUL*	TUR*	URS*	USA*	USA*	FRA*	SWE*	SUI*	SUI*	FIN*		GBR*				
Fri - Aug 7 - 11:00 am		90kg freestyle	URS	USA	URS	USA	USA	TUR*	URS*	TUR*	IRI*	SWE*	USA*	SWE*	USA*	SWE*	USA*	SWE*						
Wed - Aug 5 - 1:00 pm		100kg freestyle	ROM	USA	URS	URS	URS																	
Thu - Aug 6 - 1:00 pm		130kg freestyle	URS	USA	URS	URS	URS	URS*	URS*	FRG*	TUR*	URS*	HUN*	EST*	SWE*	SWE*	USA*	SUI*		GBR*	USA*			
Wed - July 29 - 1:00 pm		48kg Greco-Roman	ITA	ITA	URS	URS	ROM																	
Tue - July 28 - 1:00 pm		52kg Greco-Roman	NOR	JPN	URS	URS	BUL	BUL	JPN	ROM	URS	URS	ITA											
Thu - July 30 - 11:00 am		57kg Greco-Roman	HUN	FRG	URS	FIN	URS	HUN	JPN	URS	URS	HUN	SWE	HUN*	GER*	GER*	EST*							
Thu - July 30 - 11:00 am		62kg Greco-Roman	URS	KOR	GRE	POL	BUL	URS*	HUN*	TUR*	FIN*	URS*	TUR*	TUR*	ITA*	EST*	FIN*	FIN*	FIN*					
Tue - July 28 - 1:00 pm		68kg Greco-Roman	URS	YUG	ROM	URS	URS	JPN*	TUR*	URS*	FIN*	URS*	SWE*	FIN*	SWE*	HUN*	FIN*	FIN*	FIN*	ITA*				
Wed - July 29 - 1:00 pm		74kg Greco-Roman	KOR	FIN	HUN	URS	URS	TCH	GDR*	URS*	TUR*	TUR*	SWE*	HUN*	SWE*	SWE*	SWE*							
Thu - July 30 - 11:00 am		82kg Greco-Roman	URS	ROM	URS	YUG	HUN	GDR*	YUG*	BUL*	URS*	SWE*	SWE*	SWE*	FIN*	FIN*	FIN*	SWE*	SWE*	SWE*				
Thu - July 30 - 11:00 am		90kg Greco-Roman	BUL	USA	HUN	URS	URS	BUL*	BUL*	TUR*	URS*	FIN*	SWE*	SWE*	SWE*	SWE*	EGY*	SWE*	SWE*		FIN*			
Tue - July 28 - 1:00 pm		100kg Greco-Roman	POL	ROM	BUL	URS	ROM																	
Wed - July 29 - 1:00 pm		130kg Greco-Roman	URS	USA	URS	URS	URS	HUN*	HUN*	URS*	URS*	URS*	TUR*	EST*	SWE*	SWE*	FRA*	FIN*	FIN*	HUN*				GER*
		ARCHERY																						
		Individual	USA	USA	FIN	USA	USA																	
		Team	KOR																					
		Individual	KOR	KOR	URS	USA	USA																	
		Team	KOR																					
		BADMINTON																						
		Singles																						
		Doubles																						
		Singles																						
		Doubles																						
		CANOE/KAYAK																						
		C-1 500m	GDR	CAN	URS	URS																		
		C-1 1000m	URS	FRG	BUL	YUG	ROM	HUN	FRG	HUN	ROM	TCH	TCH	CAN										
		C-2 500m	URS	YUG	HUN	URS																		
		C-2 1000m	URS	ROM	ROM	URS	URS	ROM	URS	URS	ROM	DEN	TCH	TCH										
		C-1 slalom					GDR																	
		C-2 slalom					GDR																	
		K-1 500m	HUN	NZL	URS	ROM																		
		K-1 1000m	USA	NZL	GDR	GDR	URS	HUN	SWE	DEN	SWE	SWE	SWE	AUT										
		K-2 500m	NZL	NZL	URS	GDR																		
		K-2 1000m	USA	CAN	URS	URS	URS	URS	SWE	SWE	FRG	FIN	SWE	AUT										
		K-4 1000m	HUN	NZL	GDR	URS	URS	NOR	URS															
		K-1 slalom					GDR																	
		K-1 500m	BUL	SWE	GDR	GDR	URS	URS	URS	URS	URS	FIN	DEN											
		K-2 500m	GDR	SWE	GDR	URS	URS	FRG	URS	URS														
		K-4 500m	GDR	ROM																				
		K-1 slalom					GDR																	
		CYCLING																						
Sun - Aug 2 - 2:30 am		Individual road race	GDR	USA	URS	SWE	NED	ITA	ITA	URS	ITA	BEL	FRA	FRA	ITA	DEN	FRA	SWE	RSA				GRE
		Road team time trial	GDR	ITA	URS	URS	URS	NED	NED	ITA	FRA*	BEL*	BEL*	FRA*	ITA*	DEN*	FRA*	FRA*	SWE*					
		4000m individual pursuit	URS	USA	SUI	FRG	NOR	FRA	TCH															
		4000m team pursuit	URS	AUS	URS	FRG	FRG	DEN	FRG	ITA	ITA	FRA	ITA	ITA	ITA	ITA	ITA	GBR*						
		1km time trial	URS	FRG	GDR	GDR	DEN	FRA	BEL	ITA	ITA	AUS	FRA	NED	AUS	DEN								
		50km points race	DEN	BEL																				
		1000m match sprint	GDR	USA	GDR	TCH	FRA	FRA	ITA	ITA	FRA	ITA	ITA	GER	NED	FRA	FRA	NED		FRA*	FRA*			
Sun - July 26 - 11:30 am		Individual road race	NED	USA																				
		4000m individual pursuit																						
		1000m match sprint	URS																					
		FENCING																						
		Individual foil	ITA	ITA	URS	ITA	POL	ROM	POL	URS	FRA	FRA	FRA	ITA	ITA	FRA	FRA	ITA	ITA		CUB	FRA	FRA	
		Individual epee	FRG	FRA	SWE	FRG	HUN	HUN	URS	ITA	ITA	ITA	ITA	ITA	FRA	BEL	FRA	BEL	FRA	CUB	CUB			
		Individual sabre	FRA	FRA	URS	URS	URS	POL	HUN	HUN	HUN	HUN	HUN	HUN	HUN	HUN	ITA	HUN	HUN	CUB	FRA	GRE		
		Team foil	URS	ITA	FRA	FRG	POL	FRA	URS	URS	FRA	FRA	FRA	FRA	FRA	ITA	ITA		CUB					
		Team epee	FRA	FRG	FRA	SWE	HUN	HUN	HUN	ITA	ITA	ITA	FRA	FRA	FRA	ITA	ITA	BEL	FRA					
		Team sabre	HUN	ITA	URS	URS	ITA	URS	URS	HUN	HUN	HUN	HUN	HUN	HUN	HUN	ITA	HUN	HUN					
		Individual foil	FRG	CHN	FRA	HUN	ITA	URS	HUN	FRG	GBR	ITA	HUN	HUN	AUT	GER	DEN							
		Team foil	FRG	FRG	FRA	URS	URS	URS	HUN	URS														
		FIELD HOCKEY																						
		Men	GBR	PAK	IND	NZL	FRG	PAK	IND	PAK	IND	IND	IND	IND	IND		GBR		GBR					
		Women	AUS	NED	ZIM																			
		JUDO																						
		60kg	KOR	JPN	FRA	CUB*	JPN*		JPN*															
		65kg	KOR	JPN	URS																			
		71kg	FRA	KOR	ITA	URS*	JPN*																	

‡ Time that finals occur (Eastern Daylight Saving Time). Some events may not be shown live on TripleCast. Event and broadcast schedules are as of 1/12/92 and are subject to change.

*Differed slightly from current event.

Men ▢ Women ▢ Open ▢

	1992	EVENT	1988	1984	1980	1976	1972	1968	1964	1960	1956	1952	1948	1936	1932	1928	1924	1920	1912	1908	1904	1900	1896
		78kg	POL	FRG	URS	JPN*	JPN*		JPN*														
		86kg	AUT	AUT	SUI																		
		95kg	BRA	KOR	BEL	JPN*	URS*																
		+95kg	JPN	JPN	FRA	URS	NED		JPN														
		48kg																					
		52kg																					
		56kg																					
		61kg																					
		66kg																					
		72kg																					
		+72kg																					
		MODERN PENTATHLON																					
		Individual	HUN	ITA	URS	POL	HUN	SWE	HUN	HUN	SWE	SWE	SWE	GER	SWE	SWE	SWE	SWE	SWE				
		Team	HUN	ITA	URS	GBR	URS	HUN	URS	HUN	URS	HUN											
		ROWING																					
		Single sculls	GDR	FIN	FIN	FIN	URS	NED	URS	URS	URS	URS	AUS	GER	AUS	AUS	GBR	USA	GBR	GBR	USA	FRA	
		Double sculls	NED	USA	GDR	NOR	URS	URS	URS	TCH	URS	ARG	GBR	GBR	USA	USA	USA	USA			USA		
		Quadruple sculls	ITA	FRG	GDR	GDR																	
		Coxless pairs	GBR	ROM	GDR	GDR	GDR	GDR	CAN	URS	USA	USA	GBR	GER	GBR	GER	NED			GBR	USA*		
		Coxless fours	GDR	NZL	GDR	GDR	GDR	GDR	DEN	USA	CAN	YUG	ITA	GER	GBR	GBR	GBR			GBR	USA		
		Coxed pairs	ITA	ITA	GDR	GDR	GDR	ITA	USA	FRG	USA	FRA	DEN	GER	USA	SUI	SUI	ITA				NED	
		Coxed fours	GDR	GBR	GDR	URS	FRG	NZL	FRG	FRG	ITA	TCH	USA	GER	GER	ITA	SUI	SUI	GER			GER	
		Eights	FRG	CAN	GDR	GDR	NZL	FRG	USA	USA	USA	USA	USA	USA	USA	USA	USA	USA	GBR	GBR	USA	USA	
		Single sculls	GDR	ROM	ROM	GDR																	
		Double sculls	GDR	ROM	URS	BUL																	
		Quadruple sculls	GDR	ROM	GDR	GDR																	
		Coxless pairs	ROM	ROM	GDR	BUL																	
		Coxless fours																					
		Eights	GDR	USA	GDR	GDR																	
		SHOOTING																					
		Smallbore 3 positions	GBR	USA	HUN	FRG	PRK	TCH	HUN	FRG	CAN	ROM	USA	NOR	SWE		FRA	USA	USA	GBR			
		Air rifle	YUG	FRA																			
		Smallbore prone	TCH	GBR	URS	USA	USA	FRG	USA	URS	URS	NOR											
		Free pistol	ROM	CHN	URS	GDR	SWE	URS	FIN	URS	FIN	USA	PER	SWE			USA	USA			SUI		USA
		Rapid-fire pistol	URS	JPN	ROM	GDR	POL	POL	FIN	USA	ROM	HUN	HUN	GER	ITA		USA	BRA	USA	BEL		FRA	GRE
		10m running game target																					
		Air pistol	BUL																				
		Smallbore 3 positions	FRG	CHN																			
		Air rifle	URS	USA																			
		Sport pistol	URS	CAN																			
		Air pistol	YUG																				
		Skeet	GDR	USA	DEN	TCH	FRG	URS															
		Trap	URS	ITA	ITA	USA	ITA	GBR	ITA	ROM	ITA	CAN					HUN	USA	USA	CAN		FRA	
		TABLE TENNIS																					
		Singles	KOR																				
		Doubles	CHN																				
		Singles	CHN																				
		Doubles	KOR																				
		TEAM HANDBALL																					
		Men	URS	YUG	GDR	URS	YUG																
		Women	KOR	YUG	URS	URS																	
		WEIGHTLIFTING																					
		52kg	BUL	CHN	URS	URS	POL																
		56kg	URS	CHN	CUB	BUL	HUN	IRI	URS	USA	USA	URS	USA										
		60kg	TUR	CHN	URS	URS	BUL	JPN	JPN	URS	USA	URS	EGY	USA	FRA	AUT	ITA*	BEL*					
		67.5kg	GDR	CHN	BUL	URS	URS	POL	POL	URS	URS	USA	EGY	AUT EGY	FRA	AUT GER	FRA*	EST*					
		75kg	BUL	FRG	BUL	BUL	BUL	URS	TCH	URS	URS	USA	USA	EGY	GER	FRA	ITA*	FRA*					
		82.5kg	URS	ROM	URS	URS	NOR	URS	URS	POL	USA	URS	USA	FRA	FRA	EGY	FRA*	FRA*					
		90kg	URS	ROM	HUN	URS	BUL	FIN	URS	URS	URS	USA											
		100kg	URS	FRG	TCH																		
		110kg	URS	ITA	URS	URS	URS	URS*	URS*	USA*	USA*	USA*	GER*	TCH*	GER*	ITA*	ITA*						
		+110kg	URS	AUS	URS	URS	URS																
		YACHTING																					
		Star	GBR	USA	URS		AUS	USA	BAH	URS	USA	ITA	USA	GER	USA								
		Flying Dutchman	DEN	USA	ESP	FRG	GBR	GBR	NZL	NOR													
		Soling	GDR	USA	DEN	DEN	USA																
		Tornado	FRA	NZL	BRA	GBR																	
		Finn	ESP	NZL	FIN	GDR	FRA	URS	FRG	DEN	DEN	DEN											
		Boardsailing	NZL	NED																			
		470	FRA	ESP	BRA	FRG																	
		Europe class																					
		Boardsailing																					
		470	USA																				

TRACK AND FIELD WORLD RECORDS vs. OLYMPIC RESULTS • 1896-1992

For each event, the top number represents the world record (WR) prior to the Olympics.
The bottom number represents the winning Olympic time (OT) or distance (OD) for those Games.

EVENT		1992▪	1988	1984	1980	1976	1972	1968	1964	1960	1956	1952	1948	1936	1932	1928	1924	1920	1912	1908	1904	1900	1896
ATHLETICS – TRACK																							
100m	WR	9.86	9.93	9.93	9.95	9.95	9.95	9.9	10.0	10.0	10.1	10.1	10.2	10.2	10.2	10.2	10.2	10.5	10.5	10.6	10.8	10.8	10.8
	OT		9.92	9.99	10.25	10.06	10.14	9.95	10.0	10.2	10.5	10.4	10.3	10.3	10.3	10.8	10.6	10.8	10.8	10.8	11.0	11.0	12.0
200m		19.72	19.72	19.72	19.72	19.83	19.83	19.92	20.2	20.5	20.6	20.6	20.6	20.6	20.6	20.6	21.0	21.2	21.2	21.2	21.2	21.2	
			19.75	19.80	20.19	20.23	20.00	19.83	20.3	20.5	20.6	20.7	21.1	20.7	21.2	21.8	21.6	22.0	21.7	22.6	21.6	22.2	
400m		43.29	43.29	43.86	43.86	43.86	43.86	44.0	44.9	45.2	45.2	45.8	45.9	46.1	46.4	47.0	47.4	47.4	47.8	47.8	47.8	48.5	48.5
			43.87	44.27	44.60	44.26	44.66	43.86	45.1	44.9	46.7	45.9	46.2	46.5	46.2	47.8	47.6	49.6	48.2	50.0	49.2	49.4	54.2
800m		1:41.73	1:41.73	1:41.73	1:42.33	1:43.7	1:44.3	1:44.3	1:44.3	1:45.7	1:45.7	1:46.6	1:46.6	1:49.7	1:50.6	1:50.6	1:51.9	1:51.9	1:52.8	1:53.4	1:53.4	1:53.4	1:53.4
			1:43.45	1:43.00	1:45.4	1:43.50	1:45.9	1:44.3	1:45.1	1:46.3	1:47.7	1:49.2	1:49.2	1:52.9	1:49.7	1:51.8	1:52.4	1:53.4	1:51.9	1:52.8	1:56.0	2:01.2	2:11.0
1,500m		3:29.46	3:29.46	3:30.77	3:32.1	3:32.2	3:33.1	3:33.1	3:35.6	3:36.0	3:40.6	3:43.0	3:43.0	3:48.8	3:49.2	3:51.0	3:52.6	3:54.7	3:55.8	3:59.8	4:06.2	4:10.4	
			3:35.96	3:32.53	3:38.4	3:39.17	3:36.3	3:34.9	3:38.1	3:35.6	3:41.2	3:45.1	3:49.8	3:47.8	3:51.2	3:53.2	3:53.6	4:01.8	3:56.8	4:03.4	4:05.4	4:06.2	4:33.2
5,000m		12:58.39	12:58.39	13:00.41	13:08.4	13:13.0	13:16.6	13:16.6	13:35.0	13:35.0	13:36.8	13:58.2	13:58.2	14:17.0	14:17.0	14:28.2	14:28.2	14:36.6	15:01.2				
			13:11.70	13:05.59	13:21.0	13:24.76	13:26.4	14:05.0	13:48.8	13:43.4	13:39.6	14:06.6	14:17.6	14:22.2	14:30.0	14:38.0	14:31.2	14:55.6	14:36.6				
10,000m		27:08.23	27:13.81	27:13.81	27:22.5	27:30.8	27:39.4	27:39.4	28:15.6	28:30.4	28:30.4	29:02.6	29:35.8	30:06.2	30:06.2	30:06.2	30:35.4	30:58.8	30:58.8				
			27:21.46	27:47.54	27:42.7	27:40.38	27:38.4	29:27.4	28:24.4	28:32.2	28:45.6	29:17.0	29:59.6	30:15.4	30:11.4	30:18.8	30:23.2	31:45.8	31:20.8				
Marathon ‡		2:06:50	2:06:50	2:08:18	2:08:33.6	2:08:33.6	2:08:33.6	2:09:36.4	2:13:55.0	2:15:17.0	2:17:39.4	2:20:42.2	2:25:39.0	2:26:42.0	2:29:01.8	2:29:01.8	2:32:35.8	2:36:06.6	2:42:31.0				
			2:10:32	2:09:21.0	2:11:03.0	2:09:55.0	2:12:19.8	2:20:26.4	2:12:11.2	2:15:16.2	2:25:00.0	2:23:03.2	2:34:51.6	2:29:19.2	2:31:36.0	2:32:57.0	2:41:22.6	2:32:35.8*	2:36:54.8*	2:55:18.4	3:28:53*	2:59:45*	2:58:50*
110m hurdles		12.92	12.93	12.93	13.00	13.0	13.2	13.2	13.2	13.2	13.4	13.5	13.6	14.1	14.2	14.4	14.4	14.4	15.0	15.2	15.2	15.2	15.4
			12.98	13.20	13.39	13.30	13.24	13.33	13.6	13.8	13.5	13.7	13.9	14.2	14.6	14.8	15.0	14.8	15.1	15.0	16.0	15.4	17.6
400m hurdles		47.02	47.02	47.02	47.13	47.82	48.12	48.8	49.1	49.2	49.5	50.6	50.6	50.6	52.0	52.0	54.0	54.2		57.2	57.2	57.2	
			47.19	47.75	48.70	47.64	47.82	48.12	49.6	49.3	50.1	50.8	51.1	52.4	51.7	53.4	52.6	54.0		55.0	53.0	57.6	
Steeplechase		8:05.35	8:05.4	8:05.4	8:05.4	8:09.7	8:22.0	8:24.2	8:29.6	8:31.4	8:35.6	8:48.6	8:59.6	9:08.2	9:08.4	9:33.4	9:33.4	9:49.8					
			8:05.51	8:11.80	8:09.7	8:08.2	8:23.6	8:51.0	8:30.8	8:34.2	8:41.2	8:45.4	9:04.6	9:03.8	10:33.4*	9:21.8	9:33.6	10:00.4		10:47.8*	7:39.6*	7:34.4*	
4 x 100m		37.50	37.83	37.86	38.03	38.19	38.23	38.6	39.1	39.5	39.8	39.8	39.8	40.0	40.8	41.0	42.2	42.3					
			38.19	37.83	38.26	38.33	38.19	38.2	39.0	39.5	39.5	40.1	40.6	39.8	40.0	41.0	41.0	42.2	42.4				
4 x 400m		2:56.16	2:56.16	2:56.16	2:56.16	2:56.16	2:56.16	2:59.6	3:02.2	3:03.9	3:03.9	3:08.2	3:08.2	3:08.2	3:12.6	3:16.0	3:16.4	3:16.6	3:18.2				
			2:56.16	2:57.91	3:01.1	2:58.65	2:59.8	2:56.16	3:00.7	3:02.2	3:04.8	3:03.9	3:10.4	3:09.0	3:08.2	3:14.2	3:16.0	3:22.2	3:16.6	3:29.4*			
20km walk ‡‡		1:18:40.0	1:18:40.0	1:18:40.0	1:20:06.8	1:24:45.0	1:25:19.4	1:27:05.0	1:27:05.0	1:27:05.0	1:27:58.2												
			1:19:57	1:23:13.0	1:23:35.5	1:24:40.6	1:26:42.4	1:33:58.4	1:29:34.0	1:34:07.2	1:31:27.4												
50 km walk ‡‡		3:41:38.4	3:41:38.4	3:41:38.4	3:41:38.4		3:52:44.6	4:10:41.8	4:14:02.4	4:16:08.6	4:21:07.0	4:31:21.6	4:34:03.0	4:34:03.0	4:34:03.0								
			3:38:29	3:47:26	3:49:24.0		3:56:11.6	4:20:13.6	4:11:12.4	4:25:30.0	4:30:42.8	4:28:07.8	4:41:52	4:30:41.4	4:50:10								
100m		10.49	10.49	10.79	10.88	10.8	11.08	11.1	11.2	11.3	11.3	11.5	11.5	11.6	11.9	12.2							
			10.54w	10.97	11.06	11.08	11.07	11.08	11.4	11.0w	11.5	11.5	11.9	11.5w	11.9	12.2							
200m		21.34	21.71	21.71	21.71	22.21	22.4	22.7	22.9	22.9	23.2	23.6	23.6										
			21.34	21.81	22.03	22.37	22.40	22.58	23.0	24.0	23.4	23.7	24.4										
400m		47.60	47.60	47.99	48.60	49.75	51.0	51.2	51.4														
			48.65	48.83	48.88	49.29	51.08	52.03	52.0														
800m		1:53.28	1:53.28	1:53.28	1:54.8	1:56.0	1:58.0	1:58.0	1:58.0	2:04.3						2:19.6							
			1:56.10	1:57.60	1:53.42	1:54.94	1:58.55	2:00.9	2:01.1	2:04.3						2:16.8							
1,500m		3:52.47	3:52.47	3:52.47	3:55.0	3:56.0	4:06.9																
			3:53.96	4:03.25	3:56.6	4:05.48	4:01.4																
3,000m		8:22.62	8:22.62	8:26.78																			
			8:26.53	8:35.96																			
10,000m		30:13.74	30:13.74																				
			31:05.21																				
Marathon ‡		2:21:06	2:21:06	2:22:43.0																			
			2:25:40	2:24:52.0																			
100m hurdles		12.21	12.21	12.36	12.36	12.59	12.5	10.2	10.5	10.5	10.6	11.0	11.0	11.6	11.8								
			12.38	12.84	12.56	12.77	12.59	10.3*	10.5w*	10.8*	10.7*	10.9*	11.2*	11.7*	11.7*								
400m hurdles		52.94	52.94	53.58																			
			53.17	54.61																			
4 x 100m		41.37	41.37	41.53	41.85	42.51	42.87	43.6	44.3	44.5	45.2	46.4	46.4	46.5	48.4	49.8							
			41.98	41.65	41.60	42.55	42.81	42.87	43.6	44.5	44.5	45.9	47.5	46.9	46.9	48.4							
4 x 400m		3:15.18	3:15.92	3:15.92	3:19.23	3:23.0	3:28.8																
			3:15.18	3:18.29	3:20.2	3:19.23	3:23.0																
ATHLETICS – FIELD																							
High jump	WR	8' 0"	7' 11¼"	7' 10"	7' 8½"	7' 7"	7' 6"	7' 5¾"	7' 5¾"	7' 3¾"	7' 0½"	6' 11"	6' 11"	6' 9¾"	6' 8¼"	6' 8¼"	6' 8¼"	6' 7¼"	6' 7"	6' 5⅝"	6' 5⅝"	6' 5⅝"	6' 5⅝"
	OD		7' 9¾"	7' 8½"	7' 8¾"	7' 4½"	7' 3¾"	7' 4¼"	7' 1¾"	7' 1"	6' 11½"	6' 8½"	6' 6"	6' 8"	6' 5½"	6' 4½"	6' 6"	6' 4"	6' 4"	6' 3"	5' 11"	6' 2¾"	5' 11¼"
Pole vault		20' 0"	19' 10½"	19' 4¼"	18' 11"	18' 8¼"	18' 5¾"	17' 9"	17' 4"	15' 9¼"	15' 7¾"	15' 7¾"	15' 7¾"	14' 6½"	14' 4¼"	14' 1¾"	13' 9¾"	13' 2¼"	13' 2¼"	12' 9½"	12' 1½"	11' 10½"	11' 5⅜"
			19' 4¼"	18' 10¼"	18' 11½"	18' 0½"	18' 0½"	17' 8½"	16' 8¾"	15' 5"	14' 11½"	14' 11"	14' 1¼"	14' 3¼"	14' 1¾"	13' 9¼"	12' 11½"	13' 5"	12' 11½"	12' 2"	11' 5¾"	10' 10"	10' 10"
Long jump		29' 4½"	29' 2½"	29' 2½"	29' 2½"	29' 2½"	29' 2½"	27' 4¾"	27' 4¼"	26' 11¼"	26' 8¼"	26' 8¼"	26' 8¼"	26' 8¼"	26' 2¼"	25' 11"	25' 3"	24' 11¾"	24' 11¾"	24' 11¾"	24' 11¾"	24' 7¼"	23' 8"
			28' 7½"	28' 0¼"	28' 0¼"	27' 4¾"	27' 0½"	29' 2½"	26' 5¾"	26' 7¾"	25' 8¼"	24' 10"	25' 8"	26' 5½"	25' 0¾"	25' 4½"	24' 5"	23' 5½"	24' 11¼"	24' 6½"	24' 1"	23' 6¾"	20' 10"
Triple jump		58' 11½"	58' 11½"	58' 8½"	58' 8½"	58' 8½"	57' 1"	55' 10½"	55' 10½"	55' 10½"	54' 4"	52' 6½"	52' 6"	51' 9¼"	51' 1½"	50' 11¼"	50' 11"	50' 11"	50' 11"	50' 0½"	50' 0½"	50' 0½"	50' 0½"
			57' 9½"	56' 7½"	56' 11¼"	56' 8¾"	56' 11¼"	57' 0¾"	55' 3½"	55' 2"	53' 7¾"	53' 2¾"	50' 6¼"	52' 6"	51' 7"	49' 11"	50' 11¼"	47' 7"	48' 5¼"	48' 11¼"	47' 1"	47' 5¾"	44' 11¾"
Shot put		75' 10¼"	75' 8"	72' 10¾"	72' 8"	72' 2¼"	71' 5½"	71' 5½"	67' 10"	65' 10"	63' 2"	58' 10½"	58' 0⅜"	57' 1"	52' 8"	51' 9¾"	51' 0"	51' 0"	51' 0"	49' 7½"	48' 2"	48' 2"	47' 0"
			73' 8¾"	69' 9"	70' 0½"	69' 0¾"	69' 6"	67' 4¾"	66' 8½"	64' 6¾"	60' 11¼"	57' 1½"	56' 2"	53' 1¾"	52' 6"	52' 0¾"	49' 2¼"	48' 7¼"	50' 4"	46' 7½"	48' 7"	46' 3¼"	36' 9¾"
Discus		243' 0"	243' 0"	235' 9"	233' 5"	232' 6"	224' 5"	224' 5"	211' 9"	196' 6"	194' 6"	186' 11"	180' 3"	174' 2"	169' 9"	158' 2"	156' 1"	156' 1"	156' 1"	139' 10½"	133' 6½"	118' 9"	
			225' 9"	218' 6"	218' 8"	221' 5"	211' 3"	212' 6"	200' 1"	194' 2"	184' 11"	180' 6"	173' 2"	165' 7"	162' 4"	155' 3"	151' 4"	146' 7"	148' 3"	134' 2"	128' 10½"	118' 3"	95' 7½"
Hammer		284' 7"	284' 7"	283' 3"	267' 11"	260' 2"	250' 8"	242' 0"	231' 10"	230' 9"	224' 10"	196' 5"	193' 8"	189' 6"	189' 6"	189' 6"	189' 6"	189' 6"	187' 4"	175' 0"	172' 11"	157' 8"	
			278' 2"	256' 2"	268' 4"	254' 4"	247' 8"	240' 8"	228' 10"	220' 2"	207' 3"	197' 11"	183' 11"	185' 4"	176' 11"	168' 7"	174' 10"	173' 5"	179' 7"	170' 4"	168' 1"	163' 1"	
Javelin		293' 11"*	287' 7"	343' 10"	317' 4"	308' 8"	307' 9"	301' 9"	300' 11"	282' 3"	274' 6"	258' 2"	258' 2"	253' 4"	242' 10"	229' 3"	216' 10"	216' 10"	191' 2"	178' 6"			
			276' 6"	284' 8"	299' 2"	310' 4"	296' 10"	295' 7"	271' 2"	277' 8"	281' 2"	242' 1"	228' 10"	235' 8"	238' 6"	218' 6"	206' 7"	215' 10"	198' 11"	179' 10"			
Decathlon		8847	8847	8798	8649	8538	8417	8319	8089	8683	7985	7825	7900	7880	8255	7995	7482	7751	7414				
			8488	8798	8495	8617	8454	8193	7887	8392	7937	7887	7139	7900	8462	8053	7711	6803	8412		6036*		
High jump		6' 10¼"	6' 10¼"	6' 9½"	6' 7"	6' 5¼"	6' 3½"	6' 3¼"	6' 3¼"	6' 1¼"	5' 8¾"	5' 7¾"	5' 7¼"	5' 5¾"	5' 3¾"	5' 3¼"							
			6' 8"	6' 7½"	6' 5½"	6' 4"	6' 3½"	5' 11½"	6' 2¾"	6' 0¾"	5' 9¼"	5' 5¾"	5' 6"	5' 3"	5' 5¼"	5' 2½"							
Long jump		24' 8¼"	24' 8¼"	24' 4½"	23' 3¼"	22' 11¼"	22' 5¼"	22' 2¼"	21' 11¾"	21' 0"	20' 10"	20' 6¼"	20' 6¼"										
			24' 3¼"	22' 10"	23' 2"	22' 0¾"	22' 3"	22' 4½"	22' 2¼"	20' 10¾"	20' 10"	20' 5¾"	18' 8¼"										
Shot put		74' 3"	74' 3"	73' 11"	73' 8"	71' 10"	67' 8¼"	61' 11"	60' 10½"	58' 4"	55' 0"	49' 10"	48' 10¼"										
			72' 11¾"	67' 2¼"	73' 6 ¼"	69' 5¼"	69' 0"	64' 4"	59' 6¼"	56' 10"	54' 5"	50' 1¾"	45' 1½"										
Discus		252' 0"	252' 0"	240' 4¼"	235' 7"	231' 3½"	219' 0¼"	205' 2¼"	194' 5¾"	187' 1½"	187' 1½"	175' 1"	158' 6"	158' 6"	139' 2½"	128' 6"							
			237' 2"	214' 5"	229' 6"	226' 4"	218' 7"	191' 2"	187' 10"	180' 9"	176' 1"	168' 8"	137' 6"	156' 3"	133' 2"	129' 11¾"							
Javelin		262' 5"	262' 5"	245' 3"	229' 10"	226' 9¼"	213' 5½"	204' 8¾"	201' 4½"	195' 4"	182' 0"	175' 2¾"	165' 1"	153' 4½"	153' 4½"								
			245' 0"	228' 2"	224' 5"	216' 4"	209' 7"	198' 0"	198' 7"	183' 8"	176' 8"	165' 7"	149' 6"	148' 3"	143' 4"								
Heptathlon/Pentathlon°		7291	7215	6867	4856*	4932	4775*	5246	5194														
			7291	6390	5083	4745	4801	5098	5246														

w = wind-aided time

▪ world records are as of 1/12/92